cReATivity
TAKES
COURAGE

Library of Congress Cataloging-in-Publication Data is available.
ISBN 978-1-5235-0355-1

Design by Suzanne Nuis at *Flow* magazine with Becky Terhune and Terri Ruffino
at Workman Publishing

Workman books are available at special discounts when purchased in bulk for premiums and sales promotions as well as for fund-raising or educational use. Special editions or book excerpts can also be created to specification. For details, contact the Special Sales Director at the address below, or send an email to specialmarkets@workman.com.

Workman Publishing Co., Inc.
225 Varick Street
New York, NY 10014-4381
workman.com

flowmagazine.com

FLOW® is a registered trademark of Sanoma Media Netherlands B.V.

WORKMAN is a registered trademark of Workman Publishing Co., Inc.

Printed in China
First printing July 2018

10 9 8 7 6 5 4 3 2 1

cReATivity TAKES COURAGE

Dare to Think Differently

Irene Smit & Astrid van der Hulst

Illustrated by Kate Pugsley

WORKMAN PUBLISHING
NEW YORK

CONTENTS

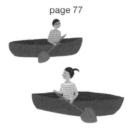

✠

To create
one's own
world in any
of the arts
takes courage.

—Georgia O'Keeffe

✠

UNLEASH YOUR
CREATIVITY

Creativity is something we all need. With a creative mind, it is easier to find solutions to daily problems. Work gets more interesting. It is easier to maintain relationships, easier to think of new ways to manage the hustle of the work-life balance, and so on.

So it's no wonder we look upon all those to whom creativity comes naturally with envy. They are the ones who invent new products, who create the most stunning paintings and sculptures, who compose and play such compelling music. But do you have to be a professional to be more creative? No, certainly not. For us, creativity is everywhere, for everyone, and inside everyone.

Creativity begins when you are able to silence your critical inner voice, and you need courage to do that. Courage to fail, courage to look at the world as a kid, courage to bore yourself to death sometimes, and courage to get out of your comfort zone.

The most important lesson we ever learned about creativity is that it is not the result that counts. It is the moment that you create (with your hands or in your head) that counts. Being there, being present, being happy to find a new solution or work on something with your hands . . . how great it all feels. So, go on—give your creativity the chance to surface. And let every chapter in this book guide you closer.

Astrid & Irene

1

DARE TO
FAIL

If you're a perfectionist, it's not just hard to look failure in the eye—it's hard to stare down the mere *potential* for failure. It can be stifling. But the reality is, some things succeed, some fail. Why should we feel shame about it? Some projects, deals, and relationships actually need to fail in order for others to succeed.

And when you do fail, which you inevitably will, it's not *that* you fail, it's *how* you react and recover from failure that defines how you move forward. Every setback becomes a part of your story, allowing you to learn and grow.

EMBRACING FAILURE. When Céline Bouton, from Brussels, Belgium, was asked by an acquaintance to organize a festival that would revive the rock scene in her hometown, she loved the idea. She was so enthusiastic that when it turned out her colleague, whose idea it was, didn't have the money to pay the sound technicians their upfront fee, Céline was happy to dip into her savings to put up the money. After all, she'd be earning it back soon enough.

When ticket sales started, only twenty were sold. But a friend assured Céline that some events sell almost no tickets in pre-sales, and still have a great turnout on the day, so she stayed confident. Long story short, only thirty people showed up. What should have been a really cool event became a terrible failure. And shortly afterward, Céline's colleague disappeared without a trace, leaving Céline to answer to the debtors. For months she lived in a state of fear, scared that new debtors would show up on her doorstep demanding their money. And beyond that, she felt intense shame about how it all had unfolded.

all, I'm proud we managed to organize an entire festival in a period of only forty days."

Belgian author Kira Van den Ende includes stories like Céline Bouton's in her book *Durf falen* ("Dare to Fail"). She's keen on spreading the message that you can learn a lot from failing—and failing is not always as bad as we have been taught to think. "When your business goes bankrupt,

> "Even the most successful people don't succeed in everything they do all the time."

Eventually, Céline decided a drastic change was needed. She quit her job and finished out her apartment lease and traveled to the Philippines, where she trekked around the country, worked as a volunteer, and regained her faith in humanity. When she came back home, she was finally able to laugh about the whole sorry mess: "All in

or your project fails, you can, first of all, learn a lot on a professional level. That is to say, how you should have done it," she says. "But you can also learn a lot about yourself and about how to take care of yourself. Failure is not at all unusual. Even the most successful people don't succeed in everything they do all the time."

A PLATFORM FOR GROWTH. We couldn't agree more. We started *Flow* magazine in 2008 and though it became a worldwide success very quickly, it has not been without its failures. In the last few years, we created some special issues that did not sell as many as we had expected. A few years ago we started a weekly journal that we had to end after a year because not enough people bought it. It was a failure, but on the other hand, we tried, and we are still happy we did. If we hadn't had the guts to start in the first place, *Flow* magazine wouldn't have been created.

And though it's important to celebrate successes along the way (like *Flow*), it is equally important to start talking about our failures (the weekly journals), too. "It isn't a very pleasant experience [to address our failures]," says Kira Van den Ende, "but failure is

very enriching. You can use a failure as fertile breeding ground, as a platform to climb up on and grow from. You've tried something, you tested if something was possible. That in itself shows courage and gives you something that people who never try anything don't have."

Arjan van Dam, psychologist and author of *De kunst van het falen* ("The Art of Failure"), agrees with the assessment. "I learned that it makes a big difference if you are focused on delivering performance or on learning skills. Your attitude determines your view on failure. Because when your goal is performance, failure is a bad thing, but if your goal is learning, and then something fails, you don't see it as a bad thing, because you learned something."

> We are far too focused on success in today's world.

10 PEOPLE WHO FAILED BIG
BEFORE THEY SUCCEEDED BIG

MADELEINE L'ENGLE *A Wrinkle in Time*, Madeleine L'Engle's bestselling and prize-winning middle-grade novel which has sold fourteen million copies since it was first printed in 1962, was rejected by publishers twenty-six times before publication.

AKIO MORITA & MASARU IBUKA Success did not initially find the founders of the multibillion-dollar company Sony. One of their first products, a rice cooker, delivered only undercooked or burned rice.

VERA WANG Wang's first career choice was figure skating, but when she failed to make the US Olympic team, she went on to be an editor for *Vogue*. It was only after she made an unsuccessful bid for the position of editor in chief that she began designing her iconic wedding dresses.

WALT DISNEY Disney was once fired by an editor who told him he "lacked imagination and had no good ideas."

OPRAH WINFREY Though Winfrey's success is often tied to her empathetic nature, she was criticized for being "too emotionally invested in her stories" at her first job in television and was publicly fired.

J. K. ROWLING Rowling, author of the wildly popular Harry Potter series, was a single mother living on welfare before her first novel was published. In her own words, "By every usual standard, I was the biggest failure I knew."

FRED ASTAIRE After an early screen test an executive wrote a note: "Can't sing. Can't act. Slightly balding. Can dance a little."

LUCILLE BALL As a girl, the *I Love Lucy* star was told that she was too shy to be a successful actress.

SIDNEY POITIER The Academy Award-winner, film director, and well-decorated diplomat failed to win over the crowds as a young actor, and was told he should go wash dishes instead.

According to Van Dam, we are far too focused on success in today's world. "We are living in a performance society. More and more is expected from people and it only seems to be getting worse. The sad thing is we are also egging each other on, so a lot of people are suffering from performance anxiety, too. But if your goal is to prevent all failures, you end up with more and more problems. One of the explanations for this phenomenon is that when you are preoccupied with preventing something from failing you are not working on making something happen."

SMALL LEAPS. If you have a fear of failure, it's hard to ignore, Van Dam readily admits. But you can still do something about it. "First, try to become aware of how it works—this is very important. Ask yourself: *Why does the idea of failure scare me so much? Is it because I'm scared I'll look like a fool? Am I scared people won't like me?* And then ask yourself if that's really what would happen. And is it helpful to think that way? Is it realistic to demand no failures, ever? No, it's not realistic at all. Next, you can look at which thoughts *are* helpful, such as: *I can make mistakes and it's all right because I learn from that.* And when you feel that fear again, the fear of failure, remind yourself: It's about learning and growing, it's not about having to be good at this or about avoiding failure at all costs."

> "Ask yourself:
> Why does the idea of failure
> scare me so much?"

According to Van Dam, people who are afraid of failure miss out on a lot, because they avoid the very challenges that make life so interesting. "It's not that you need to take on a huge challenge if that's not your thing, but anyone can take on something small, something that suits you personally. Also, if you are the timid type, and not so keen to take a big leap over a watery ditch, you'll find you become braver—you will dare to make bigger leaps—if you focus on the learning process and not on the success. It doesn't matter if you fall in and get your suit wet now and then."

IS FAILURE THE BEST THING EVER? Of course not. "When something fails it doesn't mean that it will succeed next time," says Kira Van den Ende. "It doesn't even mean you now know how to do it next time, but it *does* mean you know how *not* to do it." There are some people who, after sustaining a failure, are so devasted they can't even talk about it. But studies have shown that when you open up about your failures, you're likely to find that you are your harshest critic. Others may not even register the setback as a failure. "But you don't find out until you summon the courage to talk about it."

Like Van Dam, Van den Ende thinks it's important in these times to develop a more relaxed attitude toward failure. "Social media supplies a constant stream of pictures of people leading fabulous lives. We need to see this in the right perspective," she reminds us. "Laugh at your failures. Be proud that you tried. Don't be discouraged, and just keep on cheerfully trying."

"There is only one thing that makes a dream impossible to achieve: the fear of failure."

–Paulo Coelho

AND NOW YOU

Do you have a pesky little voice in your head that is constantly telling you what you're doing wrong? Becoming aware of this running commentary makes it easier to let it go and be kinder to yourself. The questions on these pages will help you recognize your inner critic.

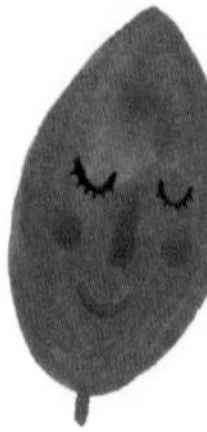

* In your mind, when did you fail recently?

* What did your inner voice tell you after it happened?

✻ How did that make you feel?

_____

_____

_____

_____

✻ Can you write down what actually happened, just the facts, without exaggerating or making
it more dramatic?

_____

_____

_____

_____

_____

_____

✱ Think about life as a learning process, with highs and lows, and remind yourself that everybody fails sometimes. With this in mind, what does your inner voice say now?

_____

_____

_____

_____

✱ Do you feel different now?

_____

✱ Do you have a friend, partner, or family member who makes the same sort of mistakes, but who deals with them in a different way than you do? Do you think that approach could work for you?

_____

_____

_____

✱ Make a list of things that you can do to be kinder to yourself and comfort yourself when your inner critic becomes overpowering.

Book a massage, pedicure, or other spa treatment.

Have lunch with a friend.

Take a day or afternoon off.

Treat yourself to coffee and pie.

Listen to music.

Stay in bed with a good book.

2

DARE TO
START

Sometimes the challenge in creating is not that there's a lack of ideas, but rather that our heads are so *filled* that we can't quite figure out how to make that first move. We insist that we need to answer all the incoming emails first or clean the desk, or convince ourselves that we need to gather more information before proceeding. But in the end, the best way to create something is simply to start. There's no need to take a flying leap—tiny steps are okay.

PLEASURE HORMONE. Cleaning your house, going through your wardrobe, putting your pictures in an album: These are all time-consuming chores we often postpone, but they keep nagging at the backs of our minds anyway. Such a pity, says researcher Loretta Graziano Breuning in her book *Meet Your Happy Chemicals*. "You don't have to finish a job in one fell swoop, you can also chop it up into smaller pieces. One advantage is that each time you finish a piece you will be rewarded by a dose of dopamine. Each step you complete feels like a triumph and will trigger this pleasure hormone. This has an important evolutionary reason: It gives you energy and the motivation to keep going. When our ancestors went looking for a water source, for example, they would have successive hits of dopamine to reward them during their quest—for each clue they found pointing to a water source, for detecting the sound of streaming water." The same goes for more creative pursuits—those first few strokes of the brush on a canvas can be the hardest, but once you've committed to making them, the next strokes will be easier. With writing, it's typing or scrawling that first word, then another, then another.

BIRD BY BIRD. Author Anne Lamott, in her book *Bird by Bird*, writes, "Thirty years ago my older brother, who was ten years old at the time, was trying to get a report on birds written that he'd had three months to write, which was due the next day. . . . He was at the kitchen table close to tears, surrounded by binder paper and pencils and unopened books on birds, immobilized by the hugeness of the task ahead. Then my father sat down beside him, put his arm around my brother's shoulder, and said, 'Bird by bird, buddy. Just take it bird by bird.'"

ALL BEGINNINGS ARE DIFFICULT. Why is it so hard to take that first step? According to Robert Maurer, professor of psychology, it has to do with fear: When you take on a challenge—large or small—it means you have to leave behind your safe routine. The amygdala in your brain (which likes clarity, tranquility, and predictability, as these are good for survival) sets off an alarm, which, to you, feels like a block. Maurer says you can get around this by taking small steps: "Setting yourself goals that are easy to reach, like meditating five minutes each day, or clearing up only one of the stacks on your desk, allows you to sneak by your amygdala on tippy toes so that it doesn't set off an alarm."

IT IS BETTER TO DO A LITTLE BIT EACH TIME, INSTEAD OF EVERYTHING AT ONCE. But once you do get started, try not to get caught up in the momentum. Chinese philosopher Xunzi says it's wiser to be like a turtle than like a team of horses. When you race toward your goal, you risk chasing right past it; if you move like a turtle, slowly and with focus, you will end up where you want to be. Feel the friction of your environment and try to keep pace with yourself—don't sprint ahead.

LITTLE STEPS, BIG LEAPS. Little steps lower the threshold to starting something new but there's also another advantage: You can do them even when you have only a little time—for example, between washing the dishes and that movie you've been wanting to see that starts at 9 p.m. There are stacks of scientific studies proving that little steps can really lead to big leaps. Reading for half an hour is enough to fully lose yourself in the book. Fifteen minutes of exercise every day has been shown to vastly improve your health. And if you listen to beautiful music or sing even for a little bit of time, not only will you be happier but also healthier and fitter. Whatever your creative medium, it's about making a practice of it. Write every day, sketch every day—what you make in your practice moments doesn't need to have an amount of polish—it's about making that practice a routine, so it's that much easier to pick up your pencil again the next day.

Maurer says taking little steps builds new familiar neural pathways. "You will soon start feeling less resistance to your new resolutions and it will take barely any

"A mind is like a parachute.
It doesn't work if it is not open."
— FRANK ZAPPA

GETTING STARTED

CHOOSE SOMETHING YOU REALLY LOVE. Maybe you've always wanted to learn French, design a scrapbook documenting your child's first years, or maybe you've always wanted to make macarons—whatever your interest or passion, make sure to choose a creative endeavor that you love. This will ensure that you don't lose interest or give up at the sign of the first obstacle.

DO THE RESEARCH; MAKE A PLAN. It's important not to spend too much time researching a project while putting off the implementation, but some research will help you to better prepare a plan of action. Remember, it's better to start off slowly and keep actions manageable.

WHAT'S THE WORST THAT COULD HAPPEN? Often it is fear that keeps us from beginning a new venture. But what's the worst that could really happen? If the worst-case scenario doesn't involve death, illness, or complete financial ruin, chances are you can overcome whatever setbacks you encounter. Dale Carnegie said, "First ask yourself: What is the worst that can happen? Then prepare to accept it. Then proceed to improve the worst."

JUST DO IT. There is a reason the sportswear slogan is so popular: It's true. Your project cannot be realized until you take that first step toward achieving your goals.

effort. What's more, it's quite likely your brain will start longing for this new behavior, whether it's regular physical exercise, ten minutes of meditating, or standing up for yourself. . . . It won't feel like a challenge anymore but like part of your daily routine."

MAKE IT YOUR OWN. "The biggest misconception about creativity is that there supposedly is this magical moment in

> It won't feel like a challenge anymore but like part of your daily routine.

which everything suddenly leaps out of nowhere," writes Erin Falconer, an American blogger and founder of Pick the Brain. Everything comes from somewhere: Any idea you can have has already been had by someone else once upon a time. To Falconer, the secret of creativity is to recognize what is genius in what other people have already done and transform it into your own thing. Her point is this: You shouldn't wait around for inspiration to strike, but experiment with what is already there. This is why children are so creative—they have no problems with copying things, and they naturally add their own twist as they play.

DON'T BE TOO SELF-CRITICAL. If you are a perfectionist, it is very likely that your perfectionism gets in the way of starting a project. Researcher Brené Brown is careful to define the difference between what she calls "healthy striving" and "perfectionism." She notes that while "healthy striving is self-focused: (*How can I improve?*), perfectionism is other-focused: (*What will they think?*)." In order to make that shift and overcome that perfectionism, you must open yourself to experiences and emotions such as shame, judgment, and guilt. By showing that vulnerability, you will also have the opportunity to explore the concept of self-compassion. "Those who have a strong sense of love and belonging have the courage to be imperfect," Brown writes. And if you are able to accept the fact that you may regularly make something that you think is not well done or beautiful, then it is easier for your creativity to flow.

"It's a terrible thing, I think, in life to wait until you're ready. I have this feeling now that actually no one is ever ready to do anything. There's almost no such thing as ready. There's only now."

–HUGH LAURIE

"Life is a dance between making it happen and letting it happen."

—Arianna Huffington

AND NOW YOU

There's no right way to begin—you have to find the one that fits your personality and particular goals. Here are six tips for taking that first step.

1. Ask the right questions. Asking yourself questions works better than giving orders. So instead of telling yourself you must eat five portions of fruit and veggies each day, ask yourself: *If health is my first priority, what do I want to do differently today?* Or instead of making yourself take breaks more often in a day, you can ask yourself: *How can I remind myself to take it easy more often?* The trick is that your brain likes questions. (Unless it's a big question that creates anxiety, such as: *How can I complete six paintings by the end of the year?* Short and subtle questions are better.) You'll feel less resistance to taking that first step.

✱ What questions can you ask yourself?

_____

_____

_____

_____

_____

2. Turn tiny questions into tiny actions. This might sound odd, but pick goals that are so tiny that they are almost ridiculous. They should require no effort at all. If you still feel any resistance, make the step even smaller. Psychologist Robert Maurer says, "If you've always dreamed about being a songwriter, resolve to write three notes a day. If you want to start spending less money, make a habit of taking one item out of your shopping cart before going to the checkout counter. If you want to move more, run for one minute every morning."

✳ What can be your tiny goals?

_____

_____

_____

_____

_____

_____

_____

3. Don't shout it from the rooftops. It's very alluring to share your new resolutions with people around you (*Tomorrow I'm going to start running! Writing! Meditating!*). But according to entrepreneur and musician Derek Sivers, it can sometimes be better to keep our plans or goals to ourselves for a while. Sharing intentions can actually diminish the chances of ever carrying them out. Talking about doing something gives you a good feeling and your mind may be fooled into thinking it's already done.

✶ Write down three resolutions for yourself instead of saying them out loud to others.

4. Be creative with time. By breaking out of some routines, you can "create" extra time for starting new ones. Do you usually settle in to watch TV after dinner? Try skipping it for one evening and see what freeing up that hour (or more) of time allows you to do. What can you fill that space with instead—bring your journal up to date, learn five Chinese words, or complete a page in your photo album? Staying off social media for one day also gives you plenty more valuable time. Make it a daily habit to exchange a routine for time.

✷ What can you trade out in order to create time?

_____

_____

_____

_____

_____

_____

_____

5. Make it into a project. Poet Dylan Thomas wrote one sentence every day—the harvest of a day's hard work—and the result was beautiful poetry. While disrupting other routines can lead to creative breakthroughs, establishing creative routines by committing to a particular action every day is a good way to stimulate your creativity, because all those little pieces can add up to something grand. This goes for keeping a one-line-a-day journal as well as for sewing a patchwork blanket or photographing your child against the same background every day. The whole is more than the sum of its parts. Read more about this in Chapter 5: Dare to Commit (page 59).

✳ Can you adapt your next project to fit into a weekly, monthly, or yearly practice? If so, how?

_____

_____

_____

_____

_____

_____

6. Make it as much fun as possible. Little steps become more appealing if you make them fun. Turn on energizing music when you're working on your new website or business plan. Brew a cup of your favorite tea before starting on that new chapter. Once you have finished one of your to-dos for the day, reward yourself with a three-minute meditation—or chocolate!

✳ What are three ways in which you can make your own process more enjoyable?

3

DARE TO
SLEEP
(MORE)

It took a broken cheekbone to wake up Arianna Huffington, former editor in chief of the *Huffington Post*, to the benefits of sleep. Before the fall, she was accustomed to working eighteen hours a day, seven days a week—but that incident changed her outlook and priorities, and helped her refocus her ideas of success.

In her book, *Thrive: The Third Metric to Redefining Success and Creating a Life of Well-Being, Wisdom, and Wonder,* Huffington redefines what makes a person flourish. "Over time our society's notion of success has been reduced to money and power. . . . This idea of success can work—or at least appear to work—in the short term. But in the long run, money and power by themselves are like a two-legged stool—you can balance on them for a while, but eventually you're going to topple over."

Her message is simple: We can be successful only when we take better care of ourselves. And, according to Huffington, the most important part of that is our sleep. In 2010, she made a pact with her friend Cindi Leive, then the editor in chief of *Glamour* magazine, to get more sleep. They had to tune out a slew of temptations, from late-night television to their constantly nagging email inboxes. But above all, they had to go against the standard belief held by many of their workaholic peers that unless you're going to bed late and waking up early, you're lazy. She found the opposite to be true: "Each of us is much more likely to be a professional powerhouse if we're not asleep at the wheel. . . . By sleeping more we, in fact, become more competent and in control of our lives." Huffington herself is the living proof: Since she began sleeping more, and working less, she has continued to be successful in her profession. Or as she says herself: "Maybe more successful than ever."

PRIORITIZE SLEEP. The benefits of getting enough sleep have long been undervalued. It may seem like hyperbole, but sleep, in many ways, is the key to happiness and creativity. Think about it: After a good night's sleep, you are a functioning, friendly human being. After a good night's sleep, you are better poised to problem-solve. After a good night's sleep, you (almost) always have better ideas.

> We can be successful only when we take better care of ourselves.

When we have a to-do list a mile long, we find it's especially hard to prioritize sleep, but it's something that has demanded more and more attention over the years. A few years ago, Astrid banned her smartphone from the bedroom, and it helped her sleep immensely. No more looking at the screen before going to sleep, no more sneak peeks in the night to find out if someone reacted to a post or message—it helped her brain wind down and relax at the end of the day. Irene is trying to do the same, but she categorizes her attempts at a phone-free bedroom as a work in progress.

ENHANCING CREATIVITY. In his TED Talk "Why do we sleep?," neuroscientist Russell Foster starts by saying that earlier generations praised the value of sleep, while in the twentieth century, we started to treat sleep as an illness or the enemy. According to Foster, "sleep is an

TIME TO PREPARE

In recent years, most people in the Western world have been
getting one and a half to two hours less sleep per night
than they should, according to neuroscientist Russell
Foster. In ideal circumstances, the photoreceptors in our
eyes absorb less light at night, causing the sleep hormone
melatonin to be produced. In bed, we fall asleep after about
fifteen minutes, and then we go through four or five cycles
of sleep, from light sleep to deep sleep to REM sleep and
back again. In the morning, the production of melatonin
decreases and we wake up.

Sleep quality is just as important as the amount of time you
spend in bed. If you're wound up when you go to bed, chances
are you will spend the night in a constant state of
readiness. Sleep is not a standby function of the brain, but
an active process that includes saving your memories. If
stress and bustle at night are causing too much brain
activity, you'll keep waking up, which leads to insomnia.

incredibly important part of our biology, and neuroscientists are beginning to explain why." Sleep is highly restorative, he says, of course, but "what's turned out to be really exciting is that our ability to come up with novel solutions to complex problems is hugely enhanced by a night of nine hours of sleep, and adults need an average of seven and a half hours. During this time, your brain is restored and repaired. As scientist Claire Sexton describes it, "Sleep is the brain's housekeeper." When that sleep is disturbed, the recovery will be less effective.

> "Sleep doesn't begin the moment you'd like to fall asleep. You need time to prepare."

sleep. In fact, it's been estimated to give us a threefold advantage to our creativity." When you're tired and you lack sleep, you have poor memory, you have poor creativity, you have increased impulsiveness, and you have overall poor judgment, he says.

Foster recommends going to bed on time: High school and college students under the age of twenty-five need at least

SLEEP WELL. It's not enough to sleep *enough*. The shut-eye needs to be quality, too. "It takes three things to sleep well: You must be sleepy enough, you must be calm, and you must need to sleep," says Dr. Sigrid Pillen, a pediatric neurologist at Kempenhaeghe, a specialist center for sleep medicine in Heeze, the Netherlands. According to her, in today's society we've had to give in on all three points. "We regard

sleep as the tail end of the day. It's something that still has to be done, but sleep doesn't begin the moment you'd like to fall asleep. You need time to prepare." If your body is ready for sleep, you can round off the day calmly and go to bed nice and relaxed. Pillen recommends putting aside your electronic devices about two hours before you go to bed. Dim the lights in the room. If you need help relaxing, try taking a warm bath two or three hours before you plan on going to bed. "It sounds contradictory," she says, "but it will cool your body down, which, in turn, helps you sleep. If you still want to watch TV, choose something not too aggressive. Avoid heated discussions, and stick to quiet activities."

In order to foster good sleep habits, keep your waking hours low stress, too. Take regular breaks to do absolutely nothing. "Brains need to first unfocus to be able to become creative," says neurologist Sophie Schweizer of the VU University in Amsterdam. That's why an idea or the solution to a problem often comes to you when you're in the shower, lying on the couch, or going for a walk. In other words, if you surrender to boredom and stop actively

"They who dream by day are
cognizant of many things which
escape those who dream only by night."
— EDGAR ALLAN POE

> "When people are too busy, stressed or anxious, the frontal cortex is overactivated and they perform poorly at creative tasks."

pursuing an answer, you may get your desired result faster. Give in to it, is Schweizer's advice. "When people are too busy, stressed or anxious, the frontal cortex is overactivated and they perform poorly at creative tasks." In a dreamy state of mind, so-called theta waves increase and these are associated with creativity among other things.

And if you still can't get a good night's sleep, a nap during the day also works perfectly fine, according to experts. A thirty- to sixty-minute nap is good compensation for any sleep deprivation during the night— and it gives you extra energy.

MOVING FORWARD. And Arianna Huffington? Since her change of sleep habits, she is now more productive than ever. She left the company she ran for more than eleven years, wrote a new book, *Sleep Revolution*, and started thriveglobal.com, a behavior-change media and technology company offering science-based solutions to lowering stress and enhancing well-being.

She's even inspired creative entrepreneurs like Jeff Bezos to rethink their sleep: "Making a small number of key decisions well is more important than making a large number of decisions. If you shortchange your sleep, you might get a couple of extra 'productive' hours, but that productivity might be an illusion. When you're talking about decisions and interactions, quality is . . . more important than quantity." In Huffington's words, "Sleep deprivation has gone from something you'd brag about in a job interview to a giant red flag"—and we would all be wise to embrace her perspective.

"When you're talking about decisions and interactions, quality is...more important than quantity."

"Have courage for the great sorrows of life and patience for the small ones; and when you have laboriously accomplished your daily task, go to sleep in peace."

-Victor Hugo

IMAGES
TO FALL
ASLEEP TO

Your bedroom should be a place where you can wind down and relax. Make it a nice destination at the end of the day: Hang art that makes you feel peaceful, set up a way to listen to music that soothes you....

Here are some inspirational images to add to your decor.

4

DARE TO
BE BORED

Historically, our downtime waiting for the bus or in line at the supermarket may have been spent people-watching, lost in thought, or simply zoning out and letting our minds go blank. But with our smartphones in hand, there's never a dull moment—we're sending emails for work, texting instructions to our partners or spouses for getting dinner started, adding events to our schedules.

Sure, they're useful, and you could fill every down moment with supposedly useful things, but natural moments of quiet are becoming more and more rare, and they are also important for stretching yourself creatively. You don't have to fill every single empty moment of time—and you shouldn't. Go ahead and waste it, because that wasted time may actually be your gain, particularly when your creative pursuits are involved.

There is a misunderstanding in our society that boredom is frivolous, that it's the opposite of useful. Because the reality is quite the contrary. It is precisely these moments—when we stay a little longer in bed just listening to the birds chirping, when we simply stare out of the window and lose ourselves in a moment, or stand in line in the supermarket staring at our filled-up cart but not really seeing anything—that the best ideas pop up. Allow

are systems in place when things threaten to go wrong. "The rise of mindfulness is one of those countermovements. Mindfulness creates moments of psychological passivity—not thinking, but simply *being* in the moment and letting your thoughts run free. Sometimes doing nothing is crucial for your spiritual health."

STOP MULTITASKING. When you do two things at once, you are actually doing both things less well, which is where uselessness can be assigned and, what's worse, potential danger. Jason Watson, a professor at the University of Utah, discovered that only 2.5 percent of people can really do two things at once without their performance in both things deteriorating. The interesting thing is that almost everyone thinks they belong to that 2.5 percent.

yourself more boring times, and they'll help guide your creative path. Here are four perspectives on what boredom can bring.

PSYCHOLOGICAL PASSIVITY IS GOOD FOR YOU. "The outside world is just so stimulating, always pulling at you and asking for attention. It makes you lose the connection to your inner self, your emotions, thoughts, and wishes. You end up being emotionally deregulated," says Jan Derksen, psychotherapist and professor of clinical psychology. But, he counters, there

IT'S OKAY FOR FREE TIME TO ACTUALLY BE FREE. Free time and the way we spend it is increasingly becoming a stress factor, as leisure time researcher Hugo van der Poel is finding. "It seems like people have taken to filling up their free time with serious activities and not including enough relaxing time." Just spinning your wheels, loafing around and doing nothing, is really useful and good for you. When you find yourself having to do a lot of things in your free time, it's not free time anymore. Sooner or later you're going to pay the

DAYDREAMING IS A GOOD THING. "Daydreaming increases the likelihood of you achieving what you want. Daydreaming is also good for creativity, because it lets your imagination run free," says sleep and dream researcher Victor Spoormaker of the Max Planck Institute of Psychiatry in Munich. Einstein, who called the process *Gedankenexperimente*, famously said it

> We make ourselves do all kinds of things all the time, usually leaving very little time for doing nothing. Doing nothing is vital for your head; it recharges you.

price. Loafing and dawdling are action verbs and it's time we started treating them that way. Don't schedule your free time full of "interesting" and "useful" activities, and don't feel guilty when you are very busily occupied with lying in the grass.

brought him more ideas than any study. Or, as trend watcher Hilde Roothart puts it, "Boredom is a good thing, because it gives you space for new ideas. In that respect, loafing about is the driving engine for change and innovation." Some progressive

FOUR TIPS FOR MORE LOAFING

MAKE IT SMALLER. Psychologist Patty van Ziel uses the words *smaller* and *less* when talking about giving yourself more space to loaf around, to slow down: "Our world has become so big, we want to know a lot of things and we also know a lot of things. The trick is to make it all a bit smaller. I think it is important to ask yourself every day: *Why am I doing what I am doing today?* If you decide to go to the theater on your day off, first ask yourself: *Why am I doing this? Does it make me happier? Or is it just because I want to be able to talk about the performance? How important is that for me, exactly? And are the people to whom I will talk about it that important to me?* Be critical about why you do the things you do."

NO MORE PERFECTION. Throw perfection out the window and let your inner slob just *be* now and then. And most importantly, don't judge yourself for it. Tom Hodgkinson, writer and founder of the magazine *The Idler*, issues the following advice in his book *How to Be Idle*: "Raise the bar. Take it easy. Surrender to happiness. Accept chaos." He knows from experience that this is what makes you happier.

PLAN SLOW-DOWN MOMENTS INTO YOUR SCHEDULE. If you suffer from the tendency to rush your way through the day, set the alarm on your phone for a few times a day, to remind yourself to take ten minutes to do nothing at all. It's okay to actually schedule "nothing."

CAN IT BE AN HOUR LATER? Psychologist Philip de Wulf posits that we should all live more according to our biological clock. "It has been demonstrated that feeling happy has more to do with how you manage your daily tasks than with achieving big success. Freedom is a huge factor: Being able to set your own rhythm gives people satisfaction." If, for example, you are not a morning person, try shifting your daily schedule one hour later for a week.

companies encourage their staff to spend 20 percent of their time doing nothing, as in: lying in a hammock, skating, a coffee klatch, playing Ping-Pong, catching flies, whatever takes their fancy. It is precisely in those hours when the busywork is set aside that some of the companies' most successful ideas are conceived of.

LET YOUR IMAGINATION GO. As for us, it helps *a lot* when we let our minds wander. Sometimes we turn our downtime into games. For example: Imagine the kind of life someone leads by simply sneaking a peek at the contents of their cart while you stand in line at the grocery store. Or daydream that the truck next to you in the traffic jam is filled with your stuff because you're moving to another state or country. Or make up a profession for all the people you're sharing an elevator with for the next ten floors. The empty time doesn't need to be filled in any serious way—in fact, the sillier you are, the freer you will be, which may open creative doors in other situations.

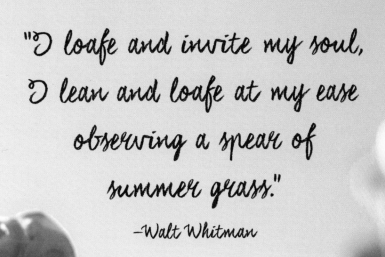

"I loafe and invite my soul,
I lean and loafe at my ease
observing a spear of
summer grass."

–Walt Whitman

AND NOW YOU

Often we don't give ourselves time—even on our days off—to sit and read the newspaper with a cup of coffee, without any thought of what needs to get done. Why not? Who told us we couldn't? Is it our own rule? How we were raised? Write down your ideas about doing nothing and challenge your own convictions.

5

DARE TO
COMMIT

One tried-and-true way of accomplishing a large task is to break it up into smaller pieces. Maybe you've heard the saying "A thread every day adds up to a shirtsleeve in a year." It sounds so simple and yet profound because approaching a project one step or one piece at a time really works.

Psychologist Leonard Martin says that people function best when they receive feedback that confirms they are reaching their target often and on a regular basis. This sense of accomplishment is built right into the step-by-step model: Every day you see your collection grow.

Are you familiar with this train of thought: "I really want to, but I don't know how, so never mind"? If you are, don't focus on what you don't know, or the effort it will take to learn. Make a small, achievable target; break it down into simple daily tasks, and soon you'll have completed a large project. Remember those granny squares? For years, Dana Beach dreamed of making a queen-size bedspread of granny squares, but just thinking about the amount of work the project required was enough to stop her before she began. Then, in 2012, she turned it into a 365-day project and crocheted one square each day. Every day she put the new square on her blog, and after three months her first bedspread was finished. She focused on small, achievable goals, and soon had an incredible work of art.

A 365-day project is a creative challenge that forces you to commit to a daily creative action every day for a year. It's the perfect way to get started. Do something small every day, and after a while you will have a complete creative project you can really be proud of. Take a picture of the sky every day at the same time to see what changes. Crochet a granny square every day, and soon you'll have a blanket. Or pick one thing and draw it; maybe draw the path you walk to work. Write a haiku a day. It could all be one big project. It could be several small projects. You decide.

Doing something every day, whether it's crafting, drawing, or photography, will

SMALL STEPS ADD UP

When making the commitment to a daily creative action, it can be encouraging to look at the stories of people who started off small and ended up with a major accomplishment. Of course, the end goal does not need to be the launch of a new company or to write the great American novel. We create because it brings happiness. But small steps toward creativity tend to expand and accumulate over time and with dedication.

DALE CARNEGIE AND *HOW TO WIN FRIENDS & INFLUENCE PEOPLE* This famous book began by Dale Carnegie preparing a "short talk." Over time, the short talk grew to an hour-and-a-half lecture. After giving this lecture numerous times, Carnegie and attendees discussed the rules they found emerging from the lecture. "We started with a set of rules printed on a card no larger than a postcard. The next season we printed a larger card, then a leaflet, then a series of booklets, each one expanding in size and scope. After fifteen years of experimentation and research came this book."

SCOTT WEAVER AND *ROLLING THROUGH THE BAY* Scott Weaver began making sculptures out of toothpicks when he was just eight years old. At the age of fourteen he suffered from spinal meningitis, his recovery from which gave him time to begin his work re-creating San Francisco in what became, thirty-seven years later, a nine-foot-tall kinetic toothpick sculpture.

SUSAN GREGG KOGER AND ERIC KOGER AND MODCLOTH High School sweethearts Susan Gregg Koger and Eric Koger founded online fashion empire Modcloth in a college dorm room in 2002. It grew to a multi-million dollar company ten years later before being sold to parent company Walmart (not without controversy) in 2017.

result in a beautiful collection of your own original and authentic material.

SOMETHING DIFFERENT. Why bother? If you are making something, for a moment you are leaving your everyday routine. Working on creative projects can replace small but worrying questions—like *Will I finish my work? Did I feed my dog? Was it my turn to empty the dishwasher?*—and give you a moment of meditative calm, place you more in touch with your emotions, and release pent-up stress. In short,

making things is good for your mind. Dick Bruna, the creator of the popular children's book series Miffy, started each day with a little drawing for his wife. To him it was an important first step to jump-start his creativity in the morning. You, too, can become creative simply by starting. Challenge yourself.

A STAMP A DAY. Some people can start a project to study specific creative techniques, like knitting, photography, painting, or drawing. Some people can think of

> You, too, can become
> creative simply by starting.
> Challenge yourself.

really original projects, like English artist Kirsty Hall, who goes on a walk each day and hides a little jar filled with something pretty she has made herself. Whoever finds it gets to keep it. This has two benefits: It motivates her to take a walk every day, and it provides a creative counterbalance to her job as a consultant. Illustrator Gertie Jaquet decided to make a stamp a day. After a year, she had a collection of 365 stamps and even held an exhibition of her work. She still continues to make them,

just because it's fun. You might have ideas as you read this that you'd like to work on. Don't be afraid to start!

MEMORIES FROM YOUR POCKET. You can make a daily creative project out of almost anything you can think of. Cynthia Grandfield didn't realize how much she would miss her eldest son when he left for college, and she regretted that she did not have more of his things to remember him while he was away. Her ten-year-old son

Charlie collects all kinds of curious objects in his pockets, and she decided to document the contents of Charlie's pockets so that when he left for school as well, she would have something to remember him by. *A Year in Charlie's Pocket* was born. She collects the little items Charlie gathers (mini-figures, twigs, elastics, notes, chewing gum wrappers), sorts them, photographs them, and puts them on her blog. "The things Charlie collects say something about him. It shows what interests him. I love recording that," she says.

"Happiness is the longing for repetition."

−Milan Kundera

AND NOW YOU

These tips will help you get started on a long-term
project—and help to keep you going, too.

* Pick a subject or theme that is personal for you and that you are
enthusiastic about.

* Be realistic about how much time you can spend on the project. Don't
forget that taking photographs of a thing or experience or posting to a blog
about that thing or experience also takes time.

* If necessary, change the rules. You can do an every-other-day project, if
every day turns out to be too much work. Just don't give up.

✳ Share your work. Posting your project via a blog, Instagram, Flickr, Twitter, Facebook, or YouTube and getting reactions from friends and followers can give you the inspiration and courage to keep going.

✳ Don't stress about it. Only think about *today's* project (forget the next 286 days or so!). A large project can be discouraging, but you'll be surprised by what you can achieve if you divide it into daily goals.

✳ Don't take yourself too seriously. Any project worth committing to for a long time should bring you satisfaction—or even joy—so have fun!

29 EXAMPLES OF PROJECTS YOU CAN START TODAY

1. Take a fifteen-minute walk every day, no matter the weather. Then write a few lines about whatever you saw and what you noticed. Or draw a map of where you walked.

2. Photograph your breakfast every day.

3. Cut and paste a mosaic every day out of randomly collected papers.

4. Pick a color. Collect items in that color each day for a preselected amount of time (a week, a month) and make a picture of them.

5. Photograph a shelf in a supermarket or local store every day.

6. Select an object and place that same object in a different place each day. Take a picture of it.

7. Take a photograph of a door every day.

8. Each day, ask a different person to draw for you a line or doodle on a piece of paper, then turn it into a little drawing.

9. Take a picture at exactly the same time of day, every day, wherever you are at that moment.

10. Every day, cut a little square of a pretty piece of fabric and sew it to the other pieces.

11. In the evening, write down three things that made you smile that day. (If three things is too hard, pick just one!)

12. Photograph, draw, or paint a picture of something that made you happy, every day.

13. Make a drawing of a single object in your home: a cup, your computer, the breadbox.

14. Document your outfit every day.

15. Record your mood in one word: happy, hurried, tired, lazy, giggly, driven, serious, emotional, feverish . . .

16. Save your shopping list or receipts from each day.

17. Write down a sentence you overheard from another person's conversation.

18. Take a daily picture of your cup of tea or coffee.

19. Draw something you've bought.

20. Photograph a street sign every day.

21. Make a drawing while listening to a song (and finish it before the song ends).

22. Write something positive on the sidewalk with chalk.

23. Make a little face out of things you have lying around and take a photograph.

24. Draw an object the way you think it will look in fifty years.

25. Cut out a picture that represents your mood every day.

26. Draw a cloud you see. (On a clear day, draw one you make up.)

27. Make an inkblot and then turn it into a little monster, doll, animal, or whatever you see in it.

28. Design a label every day: for jam, for cleaning agents, for wine, etc.

29. Make a mini-collage of your day.

YOUR DAILY PROJECT NOTEBOOK

Are you still not sure whether you can complete a 365-Day Project? Just start with a daily project. If you find you're enjoying your daily photograph, drawing, letter to yourself, or whatever you choose to do, simply keep doing it. Use the notebook on the next page to get started.

"As the years pass, I am coming more and more to understand that it is the common, everyday blessings of our common, everyday lives for which we should be particularly grateful."

—LAURA INGALLS WILDER

6

DARE TO
**TRY
SOMETHING
NEW**

Often, we focus too much on keeping things the way they are. It's comfortable and easy—but doing or trying new things can be refreshing, so why are we reluctant to do them?

Behavior biologist Liesbeth Sterck from Utrecht University in the Netherlands explains: "Everything you know is familiar, and everything you don't know may be fun, but it could also cause trouble or be dangerous.

"Animals always notice new things very quickly, and are immediately on guard. Research among apes, and even mice, shows that they look at anything they don't know or don't expect longer and with more attention. Always to figure out: Is this safe or not? It's the same for humans. It's a matter of self-protection to be on guard and to treat new things with caution." We avoid trying new things, especially the things we are not yet good at, because we are afraid. We think others are better at it than we are or that we will never be good enough. Oh, how these voices in our heads can bring us down and stop us from trying new things. But if you want to live a creative life, you have to ignore them and go for it. Sign up for watercolor painting classes, practice public speaking, or start and finish a DIY project at home. Open your mind to the things you fear and feel the energy that comes from stepping out of your comfort zone.

HABITS PROVIDE CLARITY. Our safe and familiar comfort zones are built around personal habits that make life easier. These habits provide clarity, says Roos Vonk, author and professor of social psychology at the Radboud University in Nijmegen, the Netherlands. She says everything that is automated saves you time thinking. If you always put your keys in the same place, you never have trouble finding them. And if you eat toast and jam every morning, you don't have to decide what to have for breakfast. In his book *How We Are*, British psychologist Vincent Deary writes that when we learn something new, we experience an "early awkward stage called 'conscious incompetence.' Then, with repetition, and with the aid and example of others who have danced the same dance as you are trying to learn, a little grace begins to enter your moves, a little fluency as heart and mind and will begin to work out their routine." Routines, says

Deary, make daily life possible, and, therefore, we like to keep things the way they are until we begin to feel uncomfortable with them or until something deregulates us internally or externally. "Your comfort zone is familiar and safe," says Vonk, "but when you are continually doing things the same way, following the same routine, you aren't being stimulated and thus boredom looms. Exploring new things is good for your brain; it keeps you sharp and you continue to develop yourself. And sometimes change is exactly what is needed and you have to go out and do new things that you actually find quite frightening."

Studies have shown that the start of something new is the most difficult part because it feels like a huge step, the consequences of which you can't predict. A Japanese method of change called *kaizen*

LEARNING NEW THINGS IS GOOD FOR YOUR BRAIN

"Learning something new is good for you," says Dutch neuropsychologist Margriet Sitskoorn. "Your brain is constantly growing new cells and creating connections between them, and that happens even more so when you learn or do something new." The new networks originate particularly in the prefrontal cortex. That area, Sitskoorn explains, is extremely relevant in today's world. "Nowadays we get so much stimulation," she says. "Think about all of the notifications on your telephone. The prefrontal cortex regulates your emotions, your thoughts, and your actions. You strengthen your prefrontal cortex through sleep and exercise, and this also happens when you learn something new: Cells are grown and the connections between the cells improve. As a result, you are better able to determine where to focus your attention."

("improvement") teaches you to make changes in small steps. American psychologist and professor Robert Maurer wrote a book about the technique called *One Small Step Can Change Your Life: The Kaizen Way* that deals with our resistance to change and all things new. He believes that taking big steps toward change trigger the amygdala, the part of the brain where fear resides. It can stop us in our tracks, but only if we let it.

so that you don't let your feelings dictate your behavior anymore," he writes. You can internally register the fact that you feel anxious or uncomfortable, but you shouldn't try to resolve those feelings. It helps to practice doing things that don't feel "right," like brushing your teeth with your nondominant hand. "You'll notice that it doesn't feel good, but that you can do it and, what's more, it doesn't kill you," says Vonk. "You can register the fact that

"Facing our own discomfort helps us change habits and try new things."

LET YOURSELF BE UNCOMFORTABLE. Vonk believes that you have to make a conscious effort to get out of your comfort zone if you are scared of change or fearful of new things. "Self-development means that you take precisely those steps that you find scary or that feel uncomfortable,

something feels uncomfortable but you can still just go ahead and do it. The next step is to then try this out in other situations, too." Facing our own discomfort, taking small steps, and just doing it are all different ways we can change habits and try out new things.

"Just try new things. Don't be afraid. Step out of your comfort zones and soar."

–Michelle Obama

AND NOW YOU

Study the Comfort Zone Circle on the opposite page in preparation for making your own. The things you do well and that make you feel good should be right in the center of your circle. In the first ring, circling the center, are the things that you can do well if you put in the effort. You do them, but they may make you feel nervous. The second ring includes activities and things that you haven't (yet) dared to do. In the outer ring are the things you find way too scary to try, but deep in your heart would like to do.

Remember that your Comfort Zone Circle is constantly in motion. Once you start trying new things, you will enlarge your inner circle. Your comfort zone may also shrink again if you stop pushing your boundaries. In order to track your own development over time, try drawing a circle at a particular moment and then looking at it again later on.

COMFORT ZONE

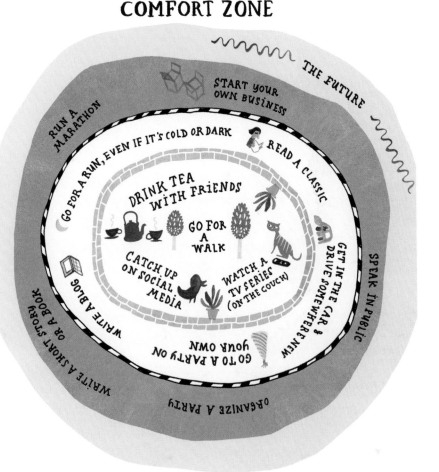

THE FUTURE

RUN A MARATHON

START YOUR OWN BUSINESS

GO FOR A RUN, EVEN IF IT'S COLD OR DARK

READ A CLASSIC

DRINK TEA WITH FRIENDS

GO FOR A WALK

CATCH UP ON SOCIAL MEDIA

WATCH A TV SERIES (ON THE COUCH)

GET IN THE CAR & DRIVE SOMEWHERE NEW

SPEAK IN PUBLIC

GO TO A PARTY ON YOUR OWN

WRITE A BLOG

WRITE A SHORT STORY OR A BOOK

ORGANIZE A PARTY

Fill in your own Comfort Zone Circle. Use it to help you discover what energizes you, what makes you nervous, and what you don't dare to do (yet). Then study your Circle and answer the following questions to help guide you toward expanding your innermost circle.

✳ Write down your thoughts about what is keeping you from being more creative.

_____

_____

_____

_____

_____

_____

_____

_____

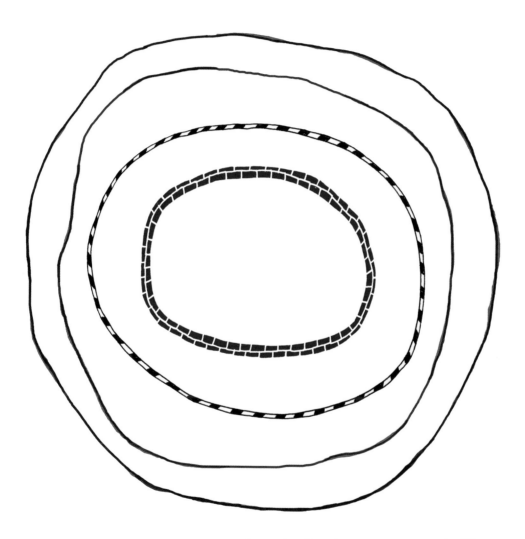

✶ What things would you like to start doing? (Think of small things like drawing, trying to hand letter one evening a week, learning guitar by watching videos on YouTube, etc.)

_____

_____

_____

_____

_____

_____

✶ Can you start this week? What day?

_____

_____

_____

* Is there also something bigger, more significant, that you would like to start doing?

_____

_____

_____

_____

_____

_____

* How and when could that happen?

_____

_____

_____

_____

_____

✱ Looking back over the last five years, is there anything that you would have done differently?

_____

_____

_____

_____

_____

✱ Are there any creative things that you did try to do previously, but that didn't work out?

_____

_____

_____

_____

_____

✱ Would you perhaps have more success doing these things now?

_____

_____

_____

_____

_____

✱ If money were no object (or at least, not so important), what would you change in your life?

_____

_____

_____

_____

_____

_____

7

DARE TO
BE A KID

"Beginner's mind" is a term Buddhists use to describe a particular state of mental openness. It means that as a beginner you have no expectations, no fixed image of self. All options are open and, therefore, you could go in any direction. You are not restricted by a set idea about what is or isn't possible, by judgments by or about certain people, or by phrases like "We don't do things that way."

With a beginner's mind, you are open to the world and the people around you and you see things as they are, without immediately having an opinion about them.

It sometimes feels like we've forgotten how to look at things without prejudice. Our heads are often so preoccupied with thoughts, judgments, and experiences that we are no longer able to look around us with the neutral perspective of a child. We see the world through a prism of our experiences and don't approach new situations with an open mind. Have you had a painful experience in a relationship? You'll likely have some issues with trust in your next relationship. Did you read a glowing book review? You may have high expectations when you start reading that book. What would happen if you were able to let go of it all and look at every experience with the eyes of a beginner, as if you've never experienced anything before?

As we get older we lose the open view of the world we had when we were children. It's almost as if the voice of experience is in the back of our heads delivering a running commentary on everything we do. We want all kinds of things, have opinions, and believe in certain ways of doing things. This makes us very inwardly focused and it's increasingly hard for us to make real contact with the world around us. The solution: Try to distance yourself from your think-

With a beginner's mind, you are open to the world and the people around you.

ing instead of letting it take you in. Sit down quietly and concentrate on your breathing. Thoughts still come by, but you become detached from your automatic impulse to follow them and end up in your familiar thought patterns. The more you practice this ability to release, the quieter your mind becomes. This will make you more open to everything happening around you and you will hear sounds you've never noticed before. When walking in nature, you will suddenly see the veins on a leaf on a tree that you've never even considered, despite walking by a million times before. This leads to new creative possibilities and alternative solutions.

Meditation isn't the only way to be more in the moment. You can also take a meandering walk (without any particular destination). Or draw, or make a slow soup, for example. You are bound to have had a beginner's mind at some time, not only when you were a child—the trick is recognizing when it happens and figuring out how to get to that place again. Margrit Irgang describes it very aptly in her book *Zen—Buch der Lebenskunst* ("Zen as a Life Art"): "It occurs to us in moments that we forget ourselves. We forget that our skirt isn't the latest fashion or that we should have washed our hair. We stop thinking about the past or the future. We have no plans and no regrets. . . . It's a hot day, cars are honking their horns outside. Children are calling something to each other. And then, it just happens. Life bares its heart, unexpectedly, without invitation."

According to philosopher Jan Flameling, a beginner's mind not only allows you to enjoy life more, it also makes you more sociable. "When you take a moment to just sit and do nothing except breathe on a regular basis, you create more space for others. It has made me as a philosophy teacher more alert, more attentive, and more considerate." It allows room for a conversation, rather than a storytelling. It allows you to connect with the person you're having the conversation with: *Are they hearing my story? What do they think about it? Are they understanding it?*

> Try to distance yourself from your thinking instead of letting it take you in.

A FRESH LOOK MAKES YOU CREATIVE. Studies at Radboud University in Nijmegen, the Netherlands, show that with an open mind we gain easier access to the secret chambers of our brains. In the moment that you no longer are plagued by thoughts rattling around your brain, your brain finds tranquility and suddenly new ideas can surface. It's the classic tale of scientists and artists who have their best insights when they're in the shower. French philosopher and writer Jean-Jacques Rousseau would have his flashes of insight while taking a walk. Ideas didn't come to him at his writing desk but on little paths in the woods.

CREATE MEMORIES. When you look at the world with new eyes, your experience of time is also affected, says Douwe Draaisma, professor at University of Groningen and author of the book *Why Life Speeds Up as You Get Older (Waarom het leven sneller gaat als je ouder wordt)*. As we get older we are no longer discovering as many new things. The backdrop stays more constant but the years feel like they are flying by. But, Draaisma says, by doing things you haven't done before, time solidifies. If you want to lengthen your perspective on time, keep doing new things, because "first times"

> With an open mind we gain easier access to the secret chambers of our brains . . . and suddenly new ideas can surface.

BEGINNER'S MIND IN 4 PARTS

1. **FALL BACK INTO THE MOMENT** Concentrate on your breathing. Use your senses: Feel how your feet touch the ground and listen to the sounds around you. Don't try to stop your thoughts, but take a step back and notice them, don't respond, and quietly return to your breathing.

2. **STUMBLING IS ALLOWED** When you start a new project, you have to learn new skills. Children fall down ten times and get up again just as often, but as grown-ups we are more inclined to stop and think: *I'm obviously no good at this.* Persevere and remind yourself you're learning something new; mistakes are par for the course.

3. **TRY SOMETHING NEW** If things get too routine, too predictable, renew the world around you. Go to a museum you've never visited before; taste an unfamiliar meal; take a lesson in a new sport or hobby.

4. **REALLY LISTEN** When we are in conversation with someone, we can be quick to form a judgment and are sometimes even preoccupied with what *we* are going to say next. Let go and try to really listen. Allow for pauses.

(first time you meet your new love, first time you sleep in your house) leave deep marks on our mind. You can also pretend: Start by trying to taste the food you eat as if it's the very first time. Savor it. Examine it. What's its texture? Which spices can you taste? The crux of the matter is to create memories, because they "slow down" time.

A photography project is a great way to create a fresh new perspective on your surroundings and see the world in a new, exciting way. Julia Gorodecky is doing that. She chooses a theme every month and posts her findings to social media (@juliagorodecky) almost every day. One day she noticed that traffic signs in her neighborhood were being "hacked" in a comical way. For example, a sticker of scissors was put on a Do Not Enter sign (the round red sign with a white horizontal stripe) to make it look like the scissors were cutting through the white stripe. These turned out to be the work of French artist Clet Abraham (@cletabraham). Curious, Julia sought out as many of the hacked signs as she could find, and posted pictures of them in order to share them with her friends abroad. It felt like a treasure hunt.

"After I ran out of new traffic sign art, I started missing it," Julia says. "That's when I came across several funny objects that just happened to be blue, and so I decided to photograph a blue object every day for a month. After that I kept choosing a new theme every month, to keep things fresh for myself."

One of the fun things about the project is thinking of a title for each, incorporating the name of the month when she can. "Since I started [this series of projects], I feel like my eyes have been opened to a new world," says Julia. "I notice far more things while I'm walking, cycling or even driving around. I'm always looking for things that can spark a theme, which makes even a walk to the supermarket interesting."

"In the beginner's mind there are many possibilities, but in the expert's mind there are few."

—Shunryū Suzuki

AND NOW YOU

Smartphones have made digital photography accessible to anyone who has one. Here are a few tips for starting a new photo project.

✶ It's fun to do a photo project together with a friend. It's not about being the best, but about seeing how you two might approach the same project in different ways. It's also fun to do if you are each in a different physical location (opposite coasts, different time zones, urban and rural, and so on).

✶ Try making a series of photographs with an analog camera, and choose how many pictures the series will be in advance—one roll of film, for example (24 or 36 exposures).

✶ There are different ways to take a series of photographs: It can be a 365-day or a 30-day project, or 10, 50, or 100—whatever you decide. There are no rules.

Make a list of photography project ideas:

_____

_____

_____

_____

_____

_____

_____

_____

_____

_____

IT'S ALL IN HOW YOU FRAME IT

Print your favorite pictures and frame them with the frames bound into this book! Or, use the frames to help you frame a scene before you take a picture.

8

DARE TO
BE ALONE

In our youth, we enjoyed many empty days—no plans, no presentations, no to-do lists (okay, maybe some schoolwork). But we could go for hours at a time without using our voices, only clearing our throats and finding them long enough to answer the telephone that hung on the kitchen wall. As adults, we tend to miss out on that luxury of spending time alone. Not only that, we "forget" how to be alone—so much so that as our children grow up, and we again face the reality of alone time, it feels awkward and uncomfortable.

But there is a moment, in the future, when the relative solitude returns—when the children are more self-sufficient, and we begin, again, to spend more and more time alone. At first, it can be startling—scary, even. It's hard to adjust to solitude after so many years of constant chatter. And, of course, there's plenty now to distract us—the white noise of social media, countless hours on Facebook and Instagram—simply to avoid the feeling of being alone. But when we spend so many years keeping our calender booked, it's important to leave some openings (or even to schedule "a meeting" with yourself!). Because when we embrace our alone time—when we dare to leave our schedules open, and give ourselves the time and ability to reflect on life without distraction or interruption—the most beautiful ideas appear.

THE NEED FOR CONNECTION. Why is being alone so hard for many people? According to Dutch lifespan psychology professor Nele Jacobs, the pain of being alone is a drive to action, which is usually an uncomfortable sensation. "Hunger and tiredness can be difficult to endure," she explains, "but hunger drives us to eat and tiredness drives us to sleep. In the same way, the discomfort of being alone drives us to seek out social contact. Humans are social creatures that don't really function unless interacting with others."

In her book *The Lonely City*, British author Olivia Laing writes about how she fared after the relationship she moved from London to New York for fell apart. She had to find a way to keep going in the city that never sleeps. "Cities can be lonely

places," she writes, "and in admitting this we see that loneliness doesn't necessarily require physical solitude, but rather an absence or paucity of connection, closeness, kinship."

Theo van Tilburg, a professor of sociology who conducts research about loneliness, says, "Man is a social being." He adds, "But sometimes people hold onto those social contacts too fanatically, out of a fear of being alone. That fear is the wrong motivation, and it's also unnecessary. 'Alone' doesn't mean the same as 'lonely.'"

CHANGE OUR ATTITUDE. With Jacobs, Laing, and Van Tilburg's perspectives in mind, it makes sense that we tend to avoid being alone. But we noticed that the constant craving for meeting and keeping up with other people made us more and more tired. Can we blame social media for this? Do platforms like WhatsApp, Facebook, and Instagram feed our constant hunger to feel connected? It seems like people all over the globe always have the same need and would like more of that feeling. That's not entirely true, says Van Tilburg. Social connection has not become increasingly important in recent years; it's only our way of making contact that has changed. "Half a century ago, families lived together on the same street, and your friends lived in the same neighborhood or city," he says. "Now

"Sometimes people hold onto those social contacts too fanatically, out of a fear of being alone."

PERSPECTIVES ON BEING ALONE

Irene: "When I was married, I loved an evening alone or even better—a whole weekend! But when we split, 'being alone' was a whole different ball game. Because while the occasional weekend was

fun, I found that being alone on the weekend and three evenings a week (co-parenting) was pretty rough going. For the first year, I did what most people do: escape. Make appointments, go to the movies, go to the bar, do fun things, and come home so tired that I did not notice that I was alone. Until I felt I could no longer keep pace with myself. Slowly, out of necessity, I began to embrace it: an evening alone, a whole Saturday without appointments, and then a whole weekend doing nothing. At first it felt so huge, so scary—by Sunday morning, I would wake up feeling sorry for myself and start to message and email people, trying to set up a get-together. But gradually I managed to stop dreading it, and now I am rather an expert at it: I enjoy time alone. I consciously plan it. I see it as a gift to myself. I can be happy in my own company, and that is a great thing that I am proud of."

Astrid: "It's a huge gift to like being by yourself. And I do. After all, you are the only person with whom you have to live for a lifetime. When I moved in with my partner and had children, it became more difficult to find time to be on my own. Every moment alone felt stolen. But I now know that I really need time for myself. To think, to recharge, and also to shut myself off from a world in which we always have to be present, funny, sharp, alert, clever, or social. It nourishes me. If I do not manage to be alone for a while, I start to feel uncomfortable.

"There are a few things I like to do alone: cycling in the dunes, going to a museum, or just spending a day in an empty house. A weekend away somewhere on my own is still on my wish list. One thing that I do regularly now is go to a matinee movie. In the past, I would have worried about how this seemed to the outside world, but now I know better. I am older and wiser and I don't care what others think. Another thing that I love about going out on my own is that I can simply take everything in; I don't need to share anything, and I don't need to have or give an opinion."

more and more people live alone, and farther apart, but thanks to modern technology, we still have contact." Van Tilburg says that the average person needs to connect with about five people regularly to have the sense that they are part of a community, and part of the world. Of course, it doesn't have to be five. "You can be just as happy with four dear friends around you," he continues. "The point is that you feel they know you for who you are. You can also have a strong bond with twelve good friends. It depends on what works for you. The quality of the connection is most important, everyone needs that for self-affirmation."

"ALONE": A NOT-QUITE-FOUR-LETTER WORD. It's not until you finally hear yourself complaining about being too busy, begin to feel that the lack of energy is negatively influencing your creativity, and acknowledge it that you can start to change your attitude toward being alone. We (Astrid and Irene) both scheduled in "alone time" (leaving free nights in our schedule), despite still resisting the idea. In the beginning, we didn't enjoy it, but we felt a bit more rested. Whoever thought being alone would be fun? "Alone." What a stupid word.

Not everyone agrees. "*Alone* is a very nice word," says Ronald Fransen, Amsterdam branch leader of the School of Practical Philosophy and Spirituality. "In Eastern philosophy, the art of being alone is the finest art there is." He suggests that one can start by considering what it means to be alone. There are a number of different ways to be alone, including being physically on your own. You can also be alone at

> ## "Decorate one's inner house so richly that one is content there, glad to welcome anyone who wants to come and stay, but happy all the same in the hours when one is inevitably alone."
>
> —EDITH WHARTON

a party surrounded by eighty people, or when you're sitting across the table from your partner. And there's another form of "alone," which is the one that causes us the most anxiety. "Being alone is annoying if you believe that it is somehow reflective of your whole person," Fransen says. "So you don't think: *I'm here alone.* Instead you think: *I'm a person who is alone.*" He continues, "We are so used to focusing our attention on the outside world and that only seems to be getting busier. There's still a lot of negativity associated with retreating from all that." It's as if we believe that our existence is validated by the number of friends we have, and the more we have, the better.

MAKING TIME. We now have these big blocks in our weekly calendar specifically for being alone—like going to a museum, or taking long walks in the dunes. We still have moments of fear about the stillness, but the more time we spend alone, the easier those moments are to deal with. Plus, there's more space in our heads for new thoughts and more creativity.

"You don't necessarily need to change your situation, just your attitude about being alone," says Fransen. "You can be alone without feeling alone. Change your attitude about being alone, and then you change your feeling about the times when you are alone."

When we spend time alone . . . there's more space in our heads for new thoughts and more creativity.

"The soul that
sees beauty may
sometimes walk alone."

—Johann Wolfgang von Goethe

AND NOW YOU

The first step in embracing being alone is to examine your thoughts and habits around being alone.

✱ What keeps you from spending more time alone?

_____

_____

_____

_____

✱ How do you feel when your weekend is fully booked with social gatherings?

_____

_____

_____

_____

✳ How do you feel when you have an unexpected afternoon or evening just for yourself?

_____

_____

_____

_____

✳ Are you afraid of missing out on something when you take more time for yourself?

_____

_____

_____

_____

_____

Block off a period of three hours this week for reflection. Meditate, go for a walk, or do some other thing you enjoy, but do it alone. Write down what new thoughts or ideas come up during this period of time.

✳ Make a list of things you like to do alone:

Go to your favorite tea or coffee spot and enjoy a cup of something warm.

Visit a museum without listening to someone else's opinions.

Take a walk in nature to clear your mind.

Enjoy a relaxing day at a spa.

Take a trip to a nearby (or far-off!) city.

Go to the movies, order a large popcorn, and watch a film you've been dying to see.

✷ Keep adding to the list.

_____

_____

_____

_____

_____

_____

_____

_____

9

DARE TO

GO OFFLINE

For creative people, there is so much valuable inspiration to find online, but the frequency with which we turn to our smartphones in mindless moments is a problem. We keep looking, swiping, double-tapping, and refreshing—even when we've told ourselves we shouldn't. Our reflex brain—also known as the intuitive brain—is to blame.

It seeks out junk in order to be satisfied, and every ping on our phones or flashing screens provides a little gratification. Offline has become the true luxury, which is why it's so important to keep trying to break our old habits. These days, we're proud if we can keep our smartphone out of our bedrooms, and in our bags while at work or in a restaurant. But even with a phone in hand, there are plenty of ways to go off the grid. Delete your Facebook app. Turn your phone off for three hours a day, just to see what's happening inside your mind. Stop reading work emails on your phone.

Do you dare? We asked a few creative people how they deal with going offline, and this is what we learned.

"I DON'T ALLOW MYSELF TO GET DISTRACTED." Dutch illustrator Deborah van der Schaaf takes a very conscious approach to her online and offline time. She avoided joining the "being online, everywhere" craze for a long time, and was successful to a degree; she bought a smartphone only a few years ago. "I ultimately caved because of Instagram and the ability to take much nicer photos," she says. But Deborah is strict with herself when it comes to the amount of time she spends online, because she wants to be able to concentrate on her work. She has very few apps and doesn't get email on her device. "I know myself and how easily I get distracted, so I just don't allow that to happen," she says. "If I have to concentrate on something I'm reading, I even turn my music off." There are exceptions, of course, and sometimes, she "cheats." "For example, if I have just posted something on Instagram, I get really curious and want to read the responses. But when I'm finished working, I intentionally leave my phone in my office and shut the door."

"DON'T TREAT YOUR INBOX AS A TIME BOMB." Online news media editor Charlie, who is based in New York City, has been covering technology for five years. He was a self-professed email addict and very devoted to connecting online so he decided that it was time for a weeklong email vacation in order to reset his priorities. "It was hard," he says, "and a bit unsettling. There's the muscle memory of checking your phone and inbox, which takes some getting used to when the apps just aren't there. But the hardest part is feeling like you're missing out on something—this sinking feeling that, all of a sudden, everyone is trying to get in touch with you and that you're

> ## "Quiet is peace. Tranquility. Quiet is turning down the VOLUME knob on life. *Silence* is pushing the OFF button. Shutting it down. All of it."
> — KHALED HOSSEINI

somehow going to be worse off as a result. But anyone who really needed to reach me contacted me in other ways. And I was able to use the time I normally spent inside my inbox doing other things, like relaxing, having face-to-face meetings, writing, and reading."

Charlie's experiment led to a valuable insight. "Frequency is where people often go wrong. I noticed that I was sending worthless emails to my coworkers to tell them I'd seen their emails. I learned that being economical with email isn't just helpful for one's inbox, it's good manners, too." But the big takeaway, he says, was that we so often treat our inboxes as these "ticking stress time bombs" that have to be dealt with right away, and ultimately our emails are far less crucial to our lives than we think.

"I PUT MY PHONE WHERE I CAN'T SEE IT." For American illustrator Anisa Makhoul, being online is extremely important. It's where she sparks her creativity and connects with other artists across the world via Pinterest and Instagram. "I often use photos as inspiration in my illustrations, and I find them online. When I was young, I would have had to go to the library for these images or look them up in an encyclopedia. This was way too much work, so I didn't do it, but nowadays it's easier because the Internet is such a good helpline. Still, being online is bad for my concentration, so when I'm busy and have a lot of deadlines to meet, I put my phone where I can't see it and turn off my email." And as much as Anisa loves all the online interaction, it isn't her salvation. What she does look forward to every

IN THE RESTAURANT

Not so very long ago, it was quite unthinkable to put your phone
on the table if you were dining out. Today, it's an exception if
someone leaves his phone in his bag. At Bedivere Eatery & Tavern in
Beirut, Lebanon, customers are offered a 10 percent discount if they
hand over their phones before they're seated. Owner Jihad Zein came
up with this house rule a few years ago, after getting fed up with
his friends looking at their phones while they were enjoying an
evening together. Zein knows his customers appreciate this policy,
because they are paying attention to each other again instead of to
their phones.

Another phenomenon in cafés and restaurants is "phone stacking," a
game that started in the United States. Everyone in the group puts
their phone in a stack in the middle of the table, and the first
person to pick theirs up pays the bill. If everyone manages to
withstand the temptation, costs are split equally.

> "You really can't produce anything of value if you aren't able to concentrate all your attention on your work."

month is Ladies Drawing Night, an offline get-together where she meets up with other illustrators who, like her, live in Portland, Oregon. "It's a community of female artists that my friend Lisa Congdon started," she says. "I have already made a lot of new friends through the group. The best part is visiting each other's workspaces. I see how other illustrators work, and always learn little tricks that I can try in my own work."

"I CHECK MY EMAIL AND SOCIAL MEDIA ONLY TWICE A DAY." American writer Jocelyn K. Glei has studied how creative people concentrate on their work in this age of distraction. "You really can't produce anything of value if you aren't able to concentrate all your attention on your work," she says. In her book *Unsubscribe: How to Kill Email Anxiety, Avoid Distractions, and Get Real Work Done*, Jocelyn offers tips on how to cope with the distractions of email and social media. "Distraction is the enemy of creativity, and email is one of the main culprits," she says. Jocelyn makes a point of checking her email and social media only twice a day— once in the late morning and once late in the afternoon. "I try to write for two to three hours first," she says. "I schedule my tweets in advance so that I appear to be active on social media without having to constantly be online. I do have days where I check websites more than I would like to. Once you start 'web snacking,' it's hard to stop again, so I try to be conscious of this habit."

Jocelyn believes that the amazing developments in technology over the past few decades have bewitched us, and we are slowly facing the consequences. "We were like little kids, so happy with our new toys," she says, "but now we are actually addicted. The tools shape us, and we are justified in wondering if these tools should be so important."

"BE UNAVAILABLE FOR FIXED HOURS." Neuroscientist Daniel Levitin, author of the book *The Organized Mind: Thinking Straight in the Age of Information Overload*, agrees that we tend to exhaust our minds with email when we could be more productive, or just more relaxed, working in a different way. "Checking messages feels good intuitively because it makes you feel like you can check off something," he writes, "but multitasking, checking your mail or phone while you're actually doing something else, tires out your brain." Although we think that we're being efficient, Levitin's research shows otherwise, and the same goes for social media. "Could Picasso have created his paintings if he always had to check his online accounts?" he asks. Successful people, according to Levitin, often have fixed hours when they are unavailable. You can train the people around you to respect your hours, too. "Just tell them: 'From 10 a.m. to noon, I'm not connected. If you have something urgent, call me. If you have something that can wait a day or a week, send a text message or an email.'" Levitin doesn't check his own email every day because he has a special email address for urgent matters, which he gives only to certain VIP contacts.

"Distraction is the enemy of creativity."

"Hang out with people who make you forget to look at your phone."

—Unknown

AND NOW YOU

Try the following exercises for one day and write down how you feel at the end of the day.

✳ Turn off all notifications on your phone.

✳ Check your messages only at set times.

✳ Take more time before responding to an email or message. If you always respond within five minutes, you create expectations.

✳ Try not to use your phone for one hour today.

Then reflect on your current phone use—is there anything you want to change? The questions below and on the following pages will help you recognize and explore your phone habits. If you're unsatisfied with your answers, also jot down a few ways you can improve upon them.

* When do you automatically reach for your phone?

_____

_____

* Where do you keep your phone when you're at work?

_____

_____

* Would you be less drawn to your phone if you couldn't always see it?

_____

_____

_____

✻ Where do you put your phone when you go to bed?

_____

✻ Do you automatically reach for your phone when you wake up?

_____

✻ What are your thoughts when you see something beautiful? Do you enjoy what you see, or do you reach for your phone to share it?

_____

_____

✻ During what in-between moments (movie previews, when you're eating out and your dinner companion goes to the bathroom) do you reach for your phone? What did you do in these moments way back when you did not have a phone?

_____

_____

_____

✳ What do you like checking most on your phone? The news, Instagram, Facebook . . . What does this bring you?

_____

_____

✳ Do you put your phone away when you're with friends?

_____

✳ How do you feel when a conversation falters because someone takes out their phone?

_____

_____

✳ After reflecting on all this, what do you want to change? What will that bring you?

_____

_____

_____

SNAIL MAIL FOR THE WIN

For most people, email, text, and other forms of electronic messaging are their primary modes of communication—and for good reason. They are fast, easy, and immediate. They can also be excruciating: When your in-box piles up, when you work all day at a computer and need respite from the screen, or when your fingers ache from the repetitive motion of typing. Handwriting (or even typing on a vintage typewriter) offers your hands a break from your computer or smartphone. Sending a card that shares a little story about what you are doing in that moment is like sending a mini time capsule. Writing and decorating it is an act of creativity. What about the anticipation of a response to your letter?

10

DARE TO
BE
MINDFUL

In his book *Catching the Big Fish*, movie director David Lynch writes: "The idea for *Blue Velvet* came in fits and bursts. First there was the image of red lips, of green fields and the song 'Blue Velvet' sung by Bobby Vinton. Then the fragment of an ear lying in the grass. I fell in love with the first idea, that first piece of the puzzle, and the rest followed."

We're always fascinated to hear how artists and scientists develop innovative ideas. Some people find their inspiration when they take a long walk; for others it can come while they page through a photo album. David Lynch meditates. He compares ideas to fish: "If you are happy with a little fish, you can catch one by swiping just under the surface," he writes. "If you want to catch a big fish, you need to dive deep. The fish on the bottom of the sea are the most powerful, pure, and magical. Those are the ones you want to catch."

What's the relationship among meditation, mindfulness, and creativity? Mindfulness can help you live a more relaxed life, but it can also spark your creativity. That's because practicing mindfulness helps us develop our ability to look and feel with all of our being. Meditation allows you to dive deep, which allows your creativity to blossom.

COUNTING GRAINS OF RICE. Lynch is not the only artist to link creativity to mindfulness. Yoko Ono claims to use meditation to increase her creativity. Performance artist Marina Abramović, most famous for her performance art piece *The Artist Is Present*, devoted an entire exhibition to it. In her art piece, the "Abramović Method," visitors are invited to live fully in the present moment. While images of earmuffs and white dresses project on walls, visitors can spend hours counting grains of rice or lentils, or standing, sitting, or lying down on crystal chairs or wooden beds with their eyes shut.

Abramović sees her performances as a series of meditative exercises. She compares the body to a work of art in which

"When you are in the moment, ideas start to flow."

Negative thoughts are deadly for creativity.

we must be present to live a fuller, more authentic, and creative life. "When you are in the moment, ideas start to flow," she says.

Danny Penman, a British mindfulness expert and author of the book *Mindfulness for Creativity*, agrees: "When you're meditating, you can feel your mind getting quieter," he says. "Thoughts still pass by, but they don't pull you along anymore. You get into a calm head space where you can observe the thoughts, emotions, and feelings bubbling up from your subconscious. Now you can also notice the softer, more subtle thoughts that you usually race past in day-to-day busy life. You become clearer in your thinking and can see all the things that are going on in your subconscious in sharper focus."

COMING OUT OF A CREATIVE DIP. It is also important to stop your negative thoughts. They are deadly for creativity, says Penman. "When you have a snide comment for everything you're doing, you're not giving creative thoughts a chance," he says. "You won't notice them or you will instantly dismiss them as silly ideas: not good enough." That critical little voice is amplified by the false assumption that creativity is something you either have or you don't.

According to Penman, mindfulness will help you step out of your whirlwind of thoughts. "You learn that your inner voice doesn't always have to be right," he says. "The fact that you are thinking something doesn't mean it's true. Thoughts are not facts, even if some do a good job at

WHY MINDFULNESS IS SO GOOD FOR YOU

Mindfulness is a kind of training that teaches us to accept being in the here and now. It may sound easy, but it's not. Our thoughts wander easily to the past and to the future—we keep revisiting experiences, and we're also concerned about events that haven't happened yet. We seem to constantly go over and over the same considerations. Mindfulness helps us get "off the treadmill of our thoughts, and look into the world with our eyes open," says psychologist and mindfulness trainer Rob Brandsma. "What do our senses tell us right now, in this moment?"

The goal, of course, isn't to eliminate thinking, according to Brandsma: "Our minds have an amazing capacity to solve problems and to strategize for the things we need in our lives. Mindfulness teaches you how to grab the controls. We can consciously choose to dream about a fantasy, or to philosophize. But we can also choose to gently ignore a worrisome thought, or save it for a little while. There is nothing wrong with thinking, but the key is to choose consciously."

claiming they are. Sometimes it takes awhile before you can look at your thoughts with some distance. But once you've experienced what that feels like, it's an enormous liberation. The realization that you are not your thoughts and that you don't have to listen to the voice that says you aren't good enough, clears the path for creativity."

When a foolish and counterproductive thought passes by, you can choose to ignore it. You can step out of this obstructive and

BREAKING PATTERNS. Rising above your thoughts is just one of the methods mindfulness can teach you; there are many more ways to break your destructive patterns. "People are creatures of habit," Penman says. "Our brain is very good at creating routines and patterns. When you have done something a few times, a routine starts to form in your brain; a habit is born. This has its uses. It saves a lot of time if you can outsource certain tasks to autopilot

> **"Mindfulness can put a kind of spam filter on your mind."**

destructive spiral of thoughts and regain control over your direction. When you do this, you are no longer trapped by thoughts that strangle every creative impulse. It lets you relax. As American mindfulness trainer Ilene Gregorian says, "Your own thoughts are able to take you down quicker than any enemy. Mindfulness can put a kind of spam filter on your mind."

and don't have to think about each step you take throughout the day. But the disadvantage is that you tend to always follow the same paths in your thoughts and approach things in the same way all the time. In the long run you become unable to even imagine there might be a different way to solve a problem: *But this is how I always do it.*"

Mindfulness challenges you to break

through your patterns in your thoughts and life. It prompts you again and again to be alert. *What's happening? What impulses am I feeling? And how can I do it differently?* Looking at things afresh and asking questions are at the core of the creative process.

FIFTEEN MINUTES EARLY. How do you translate theory into practice? Is it really necessary to meditate? "It is very handy if you do, and it doesn't have to take a lot of time," Penman says. "In my book I advise people to do a ten-minute meditation twice a day. The morning is the best time for one of those moments, and you could build in a fixed moment at the end of your workday for the second one. If you have to, go to bed a bit earlier in the evenings, and wake up early enough to do the meditation before you go to work; that way it doesn't take away from your night's rest. It takes some getting used to in the beginning, but once it's become a part of your routine, it's easier to keep it up and it prevents procrastination."

A DIFFERENT PATH. Remember, mindfulness is not a magic bullet. If you sit and meditate with the express purpose of being creative *now*, it's likely nothing will happen. "After ten minutes of meditating, [*Mulholland Drive*] was suddenly there," David Lynch writes. "Strung together like pearls on a necklace, the ideas came to me for the beginning, middle, and end of the movie. I felt grateful. But it was the only time ever that this has happened during a meditation. You can't see it as a quick way to score good ideas. It comes through another path. What meditation does is enlarge your conscious mind. It leaves you feeling refreshed and full of new energy, hungry to get back to work and to notice the new creative ideas."

"A calm mind
is a
creative mind."
—Unknown

AND NOW YOU

The Three-Minute Breathing Space is an easy exercise you can fit between the other things in your busy day.

1. Take one minute to make a "weather report." Tell yourself how things are inside you right now: your thoughts, your body, your feelings, and your mood. Only observe; do not change anything.

2. In the second minute, start paying close attention to your body: Is there any tension anywhere? Where can you feel your breathing most clearly? Nose, chest, stomach? Focus your attention on that spot for a minute.

3. Slowly expand your attention by allowing your breath to travel through your whole body. At the end of the three minutes, notice the place where you are sitting and the space around you. Take it in with all your senses.

11

DARE TO

NOURISH
YOURSELF

If you want to be creative, you need to fill yourself with inspiration. Treat your eyes to visual candy and the thoughts in your mind will begin to fit together in new ways. Make time to visit a bookstore (our favorite: the children's shelves), or go to a museum, or sit in a cafe and people-watch, or rent a bike and ride through your neighborhood for a different perspective. This is how the inspiration process works for us, but it can be quite different for every person. Engage your senses by trying new activities and immersing yourself in different environments, and you'll begin to discover what inspires you most.

It's so important to block off time to "feed" ourselves—to take ourselves on a creative date of sorts—yet often this gets bumped to the bottom of the priority list. There's always more work waiting or a pile of clothes that need to be washed. But just as a physical body functions best when fed with the right nutrients, the creative mind needs a certain kind of nourishment, too—and if you don't feed your creativity, if you keep it at the bottom of your to-do list, your work and your work process can weaken.

> **Inspiration is so unique to each individual.**

Mindfulness expert Danny Penman confirms that a solo date should be a permanent fixture on everyone's schedule. The activity can be anything: visiting an art gallery, going mountain climbing, driving a different route, or even walking through a new city. "Take the time and space to allow yourself to be surprised by serendipity," he says. "It's not only relaxing but also gets your creative juices flowing."

Penman calls it a "creative date" because your creativity is engaged whenever you step out of your daily routine and do something fun. "Anything that's new—a museum exhibition or a workshop in watercolor painting, flower arranging, whatever—helps to get you thinking outside of the box," he says, "while you are also being fed new ideas, knowledge, and images."

And yet, trying something new is not enough—relaxing your mind, says Penman, is equally important in feeding yourself artistically. When you are meditating, sitting on a bench outdoors, or walking into a new room in a museum, your brain begins to relax, allowing it to process information and associate freely. Later on, those ideas will bubble up from your subconscious. It's the classic tale of scientists and artists discovering their most brilliant insights in the moments when they weren't focusing at all. As Mozart wrote in one of his letters: "When I am, as it were, completely myself, entirely alone, and of good cheer—say traveling in a carriage, or walking after a good meal, or during the night when I cannot sleep—it is on such occasions that my ideas flow best, and most abundantly."

THE ARTIST'S WAY. Julia Cameron, in her book *The Artist's Way*, concurs, calling her exercise the "the artist date." When journalist Caroline Buijs took a course based on *The Artist's Way,* she initially thought she was "being given permission to hit the town with a wildly attractive sculptor, but this is unfortunately not the case." An artist date, not unlike the creative date Penman describes, is something you do by yourself and requires that you free up time every week to feed your creative awareness. Because inspiration is so unique to each individual, there are many ways of finding it in everyday life. You do this by taking in and storing new images, and paying attention to details—trying a new route during a walk, for example. This could also be spending a few hours taking pictures in the city,

looking at art books, or leisurely browsing in a secondhand store.

"During class, each of us came up with ten ideas for an artist date and shared them with the group," Buijs explains. "So we all went home with a list of forty ideas. For my first date, I walked around a part of town I'm not familiar with,

SEE, THINK, WONDER

When you are going to an art museum for inspiration, it's good to try a new approach to looking at the art. Harvard University developed a viewing strategy called See/Think/Wonder that's designed to help you see more.

1. Stand in front of a painting or sculpture and attentively look at what you see, without thinking about what it means. This might sound logical, but we often tend to overlook the details.

2. Examine what you are thinking and feeling about the artwork.

3. Ask yourself questions. What might the artist have been feeling while he/she painted the work? What was he/she trying to portray?

slowly and attentively studying the details on façades and tiles. I realized that this was actually similar to the walks I used to take with my children when they were little. They would also stop and stand still end-

postcards, filled her pockets with shells, and collected scraps of fabric, ribbons, and paper. "This brought me much closer to creativity, and it literally becomes more of an everyday thing," she says.

> Nature and art can give you a feeling of transcendence.

lessly during these walks, even though all they were studying were hubcaps on cars and spokes on bikes."

Another important lesson is that hobbies are useful in the search for inspiration because they "stimulate the artistic brain [which can] also lead to enormous creative breakthroughs." *The Artist's Way* also suggests doing something every day that stimulates our creativity. Caroline cut out pictures of messy interiors, bought pretty

NOTICING YOUR PATTERNS. According to philosopher Mieke Boon, art has a meditative power. "Nature and art can give you a feeling of transcendence, can make you feel like you are rising above your daily troubles, and then a great sense of peace comes over you," she writes in De filosofie van het kijken (*The Philosophy of Looking*). "Your

thoughts stand still for a moment and you only 'are.' It's very nice when your thoughts stop for a moment. But it's when the thinking and the judging start up again that you can examine so much. That's the most important part of meditation. You gain more insight into the way you think, feel, and observe. And looking at art can help achieve all that."

After taking herself on a creative date, journalist and psychologist Otje van der Lelij noticed that the art that speaks to her most is created by artists who threw out the rule book and any social conventions. She connected this observation to her own life when she read *The Wonderbox* by cultural historian Roman Krznaric. "Many artists conformed to the times they lived in. We do the same, in principle," Krznaric writes. Otje began to realize

why she finds the art that doesn't conform so interesting. "Daring to be different has always been a central theme in my life. As a young girl I was a huge fan of Pippi Longstocking, who was bold enough to be different, who slept with her feet on her pillow so she could wiggle her toes freely, and who lived all on her own in Villa Villekulla. Pippi was my great role model: She had the spirit of an artist, and I'm still a big fan of her. I sometimes let myself be too influenced by what other people think and feel. What if I let go of that from now on? Even when dozens of people are watching me? That's how I want to live my life. A free spirit, thinking outside of the box. Or as Astrid Lindgren wrote about Pippi: 'Pippi doesn't live by anyone's rules but her own, and she's perfectly fine with being a little different.'"

Otje's creative experiment ends with a resolution that can apply to everyone: "I'm

> **"I sometimes let myself be too influenced by what other people think and feel."**

going to make a point of going on creative dates with myself more often, but it should also be possible to be creative all the time and everywhere. It's a way of life: staying open-minded, authentic, and full of passion. Hey, isn't that a resolution we all want to live by?"

ACTIVITY NIGHTS. A fun and cozy way to nourish yourself is to organize a themed activity night. It could be a cozy knitting circle, a painting party, or a drawing night. "Many people have the desire to do something creative, but they need the encouragement—and maybe even a little pressure—that you get from a group event,"

says illustrator and artist Courtney Cerruti. Courtney teaches classes on everything from making zines to painting chocolates, and for the last three years, she has also been organizing Social Sketch nights, which are now held all over the United States. "During these events, you work on different sketches as a group," Courtney says. "The advantage of this over a class is that you are not required to learn anything or pay attention. You can just draw and chat with the others. And it does give you that added push to actually do something. Sometimes it's hard to get motivated when you're just home alone."

When Courtney organized the first Social Sketch event some years ago with a fellow illustrator, she didn't expect it to be such a success. Now she understands why it took off. "I have noticed that so many people have a deep-seated desire to create something," she says. "We spend so much time at our computers, and creativity has been undervalued for so long. Social Sketch makes it really easy to start drawing again. We just grab some markers, paints and pencils, and popcorn and wine; that's it."

"We must never stop dreaming. Dreams provide nourishment for the soul, just as a meal does for the body."

—Paulo Coelho

HOW TO ORGANIZE YOUR OWN DRAWING NIGHT

While your activity night doesn't have to be drawing-themed, it is a low-pressure way to start since the materials are inexpensive and easy to find. Paper and pencils are all you need, and you can always scale it up to include markers, colored pencils, pens, watercolors—and snacks, of course!

1. Invite some friends you'd like to draw with. If this is your first time hosting, perhaps limit the guest list to the people you feel most comfortable with.

2. Stock up on drinks and snacks. It doesn't have to be too complicated. Put everything out on the table.

3. Lay out all the drawing supplies so everyone can share. This is a great way to try a new paint or discover your new favorite pen.

4. Choose a drawing theme. Not only does it help you get started, but it's interesting to see other people's interpretations of the same theme. You also might choose a color palette (three or four colors that everyone will be working with). Limitations can actually stimulate creativity.

5. Talk about your work as you draw. One of the best parts about a drawing night is hearing other people's tips and opinions.

6. At the end of the evening, lay all the drawings on the table and discuss them. You'll notice that your skills will improve with every drawing night!

DRAWING NIGHT THEMES

* Botanical   * People
_____   _____

* Abstract   * Collage
_____   _____

* Fashion   * Patterns
_____   _____

* In and around the house   * Black and white
_____   _____

_____

_____

_____

_____

_____

_____

Feeling inspired to take yourself on a creative date? Here are a few ideas.

✻ Make a dream list of museums you want to visit around the world.

_____

_____

_____

_____

✻ Make a list of local museums or exhibits that are easy to visit, and set a date with yourself to do so. Write down the dates in your planner.

_____

_____

_____

_____

✽ Other solo creative date ideas:

Take a workshop or class.

Watch a movie at an arthouse movie theater.

Spend time browsing in a bookstore.

See a play.

Attend a lecture given by a writer or artist.

Look at beautiful photographs in a magazine.

Read at the library for a few hours.

12

DARE TO
BE QUIET

Life is always hectic. So what do you do when your head is spinning with to-dos, deadlines, and daily chores, and there is no room left for being creative? The thing we've discovered that helps us best is very simple: silence. No children asking questions about what we're having for dinner that evening, no beeping phones, no meetings, no radio. Just nothing.

Silence used to be a somewhat scary thing to us. Almost ten years ago, we both completed an eight-week-long Mindfulness-Based Stress Reduction course. Included in the program was a silent day, in which participants who share the space together for the entirety of the retreat speak not a word for a given amount of time—in this case, a day. We were both a little bit reluctant to take part in the silent day—the concept felt very uncomfortable to us. Maybe because we were afraid of all the thoughts that would drift into our heads when there were no distractions for hours. We both approached that day with a little pain in our stomachs, but by the end of the day we had learned that silence is a beautiful thing. We felt much more relaxed, our minds were clearer, it felt like our hard drives were emptied a bit and there was more lightness all over.

These days, we try to incorporate more silence into our routines by regularly going cycling or walking in the dunes near our

houses. Birds are always chirping, but the sounds of nature have the same effect on us as that silent day. We explored a few different ways to enjoy silence and their instantly calming effects.

SILENT RETREAT. Attending a silent retreat for a weekend or for five days (even better, it seems!) has been on our bucket list ever since we experienced that first silent day. To explore the idea further, we asked journalist Irene Ras to attend one and write about it for *Flow* magazine. She went to a monastery in a little town in the Netherlands, where eight Dominican brothers live together and have an attic that is used for silent retreats. She wrote: "The first hours of not speaking are okay, but then I fear the many hours of silence lying in wait. The early-morning meditation and silent breakfast don't switch off my thoughts as I had hoped. I reexperience

everything that has happened, all the feelings I've had, over the past week. And in the second meditation I ask myself if my head will ever stop mulling about it all again. Where, then, is that silence when you have opened yourself up to it? Then I realize during a walk that I am already in that silence and that the real worrying has eased. The big thoughts still pop up, but not all of them are that scary."

JOURNALING. Although a silent retreat is a good way to find new inspiration and perspective, it is not necessary to leave your house to find those same things. A simple way that we find inner silence is keeping a diary. Christine de Vries is a writing coach who has taught courses in creative diary writing since 1993. Keeping a diary, she says, enables you to see your life in a broader way. For her, a diary is not just a notebook, but a special place to keep her thoughts and a workplace for reflection in language and pictures. "I love the word for this—*journaling*, the habit of keeping a diary every day," De Vries says. "When you

> **"When you write, you take time to think about what is going on inside you."**

write, you take time to think about what is going on inside you. This can be your thoughts or your feelings. Journaling is a method for creative reflection and increased awareness, and it doesn't matter if you are a good writer or if your spelling is perfect. It's not for anyone to read: It doesn't matter what anyone would think of it. The important thing is to describe what is going on in you and what happens with that feeling while you write. I am often amazed by the creativity that surfaces in the process."

MEDITATION. To increase the silence in our daily lives, we've also both started doing regular meditations. It has been scientifically proven that just sitting in silence and bringing attention to your breath leads to more relaxation. Mark Williams,

mindfulness expert and professor of clinical psychology at Oxford University, agrees. "We seem to think that being busy and rushing around means we are very creative and productive," he says. "In actual fact, this is a situation in which our brains are in 'flight mode' the whole time. If you were to put someone who is always busy in a brain scanner and looked at their amygdala, you would see that it is chronically overactive. The amygdala is the part of the brain that is involved in our fight-or-flight responses. You can only break the pattern of this chronic overactivity by taking regular breaks and making conscious choices."

SILENCE, PLEASE

We live in a world full of constant noise—the sounds of traffic and sirens on the street, the chatter and background music in a café, the consistent hum of a refrigerator, the beeping and buzzing from phone notifications. In Finland, space, time, peace, and quiet are recognized as essential elements lacking in our everyday, modern lives. In an effort to boost the country's tourism in 2010, delegates decided the most attractive attribute Finland offered to travelers was the tranquil silence found in nature, and thus, the "Silence, Please" campaign was born. The campaign encourages people to "take in the sound of quiet" and to "hear yourself think," whether that's achieved by relaxing in a sauna, bird-watching, fishing, or staying in a snug log cabin deep in the forest.

While the "Silence, Please" campaign has brought increased tourism to Finland, following the principles of this idea on a daily basis can heighten our physical and mental health. In the *Proceedings of the National Academy of Sciences*, a study was published that found adults who walked in silence regularly experienced brain growth in the hippocampus—the part of the brain associated with memory, the ability to learn, and emotions. Regular moments of silence have also been shown to improve sleep disorders, lower blood pressure, and reduce stress.

In other words, you go from *doing* to *being*. To us, meditating is a great way to enjoy silence every day, and it helps bring our minds to rest during busy times. Our next plan: Not only meditate in the morning, but also when we come home. And if the children jump on us, asking what's for dinner, we will say: I will tell you, after my quiet moment upstairs.

TAKING A BREAK. Aside from necessary sleep (see Chapter 3), our brain and our body need time to recharge from time to time, and there are several ways to reclaim that quiet space. Maybe you recognize this scenario: You're busy at a task—furiously working at your easel, typing away at a report, or practicing a chord progression— and even though you feel the need to stop for a while, the thought *I'll just do this first* persists. Ask yourself whether it is really necessary to complete that task at that moment. Wouldn't it be healthier to stop for a bit? Taking a small breather doesn't mean you're not doing anything.

Another way to invite quiet, introspective moments into your daily routine when

"We seem to think that being busy and rushing around means we are very creative and productive."

your headspace feels a little chaotic is to shut down your TV and social media for a week (see also Chapter 9: Dare to Go Offline). "Switching off," even for just a few days, will give you more time than you think is possible.

REVELING IN THE WAIT. The next time your colleagues or friends are running late to meet you, try viewing it as an opportunity. It's easy to be annoyed that they're wasting your time, but quiet moments like these are also perfect for mini-meditation. Embrace it: Take a short walk, focusing all your attention on your feet, without a concrete goal in mind. Daydreaming during the wait helps stop negative thoughts from gaining the upper hand, and at the same time stimulates creativity.

REFLECTION. Jon Kabat-Zinn, founder of the mindfulness movement and author of *Letting Everything Become Your Teacher: 100 Lessons in Mindfulness*, recognizes the importance of making time to reflect on your day. "Mindfulness doesn't mean you push your thoughts away or close yourself off to them to 'clear your mind.' You don't have to try to stop the thoughts that run through your mind like a waterfall. Just make some room for them, take note of them and recognize them for what they are, thoughts, and leave them be."

"Our greatest experiences are our quiet moments."

–Friedrich Nietzsche

AND NOW YOU

Coloring is such a great way to stop your thoughts for a while. It offers mindful relief without the paralysis sometimes caused by a blank page. It's a creative distraction that's also satisfyingly productive—just think how rare it is to be able to create something tangible and nice-looking at a fairly predictable pace in a relatively short amount of time! Try your own hand at it with pens or colored pencils on these black-and-white coloring pages made by illustrator Anisa Makhoul.

KEEP A
QUIETNESS
DIARY

Mindfulness means frequently taking a step back. It's a constant impulse to be alert. What's going on? How am I doing? We get distracted so easily, and it's worth structuring some time and space to really focus yourself. Start a diary about your sensory experiences, in which you write every day about at least one moment that you were completely present with your attention. You don't have to write a long story; just a few words are enough. Use your quietness diary to record an experience that you wouldn't ordinarily notice. Try closing your eyes, and listen to sounds you regularly block out (a quietness diary doesn't need to be made in silence—rather, it's about quieting your mind). Use your nose to appreciate the scent as you pass by the bakery, or even the not-so-nice smell that lingers in the wake of the sanitation truck. Doing these daily exercises primes your ability to pay attention and focus.

**"Life changes in the instant.
The ordinary instant."**
—JOAN DIDION

13

DARE TO

TEAM
UP

You've started practicing mindfulness. You've boosted your energy levels, gained confidence in your abilities, and started creating. But now you want to find a community of people like you who can appreciate you and your art. You want to talk about your ideas, to sit with a latte in your favorite café and let ideas flow. You want a creative partner.

When you find the right partner, creating is so much easier. They will help you develop your ideas, hone your skills, and master your craft. "Sometimes you meet someone who could change your life," writes author and historian Joshua Wolf Shenk in his book, *Powers of Two: How Relationships Drive Creativity.* "Sometimes you feel that possibility. The sense that, in the presence of this celestial body, you fall into a new orbit; that the ground beneath you is more like a trampoline; that you might be able—with this new person—to create things more beautiful and useful, more fantastic and more real, than you ever could before."

Think of all the creative duos who have transformed the world around us: musicians like John Lennon and Paul McCartney and André 3000 and Big Boi, fashion designers Viktor and Rolf, scientists Marie and Pierre Curie and Francis Crick and James D. Watson, comedians Keegan-Michael Key and Jordan Peele,

photographers Inez van Lamsweerde and Vinoodh Matadin, Scandinavian "knitting boys" Arne & Carlos. There are so many creative duos from the past and the present who have made inspiring art, music, comedy, dance, and scientific discoveries that partnership starts to look like a primary force in the creative world.

THE CREATIVE CONNECTION. Shenk is fascinated by people who produce extraordinary creative works together, and began both a personal and professional

quest to explore the subject of creative pairs.

"When it comes to connection, I know I'm not alone in wanting more," he writes. "Even accomplished people hunger to be part of that equation in which one and one makes infinity." He called that lightning bolt of creative connection "energizing friction."

Shenk then went in search of that elusive connection. He researched the lives of famous creative partners, interviewing them or people who knew and worked with them, and tried to examine how and why that lightning bolt hits when it does.

After studying creative partnerships for more than five years, Shenk determined that there are many kinds of creative partnerships. The first, and most obvious, are like those listed on pages 189–90. We know their names, how they worked together, and

Although a working creative partnership must inherently have some overlapping interests, Shenk says that they also must be different enough to "charge" one another up, and sometimes conflict is a good thing. "One way to identify these pairs is to see that they have extreme difference and extreme similarity at the same time."

Creative duos often find each other through their shared interests.

what they produced. Shenk realized that they often found each other through their shared interests: They hung out in the same environments, loved a certain kind of music, or had mutual friends. This may all seem simple, but it's crucial: The setting in which partners meet can determine a great deal about how they connect and what kind of connection they're seeking.

John Lennon and Paul McCartney, for example, were very different people, with very different personal styles, but they shared their love of music. As with so many successful creative pairs, they didn't always like each other. They were competitors, constantly trying to create something better, something more mind-blowing than the other could. There was tension

ARNE & CARLOS, THE "KNITTING BOYS" OF SCANDINAVIA

Scandinavian designers Arne Nerjordet and Carlos Zachrison are the creators of ARNE & CARLOS, a fashion brand based around their love of knitting and knitwear. They've gained worldwide fame with their books *55 Christmas Balls to Knit*, *Knitted Dolls*, and *Knit-and-Crochet Garden*, all of which are bestsellers.

HOW DOES THE MAGIC BETWEEN YOU TWO WORK?
Carlos: We are quite good at reading each other's minds. If one of us has an idea, the other one easily picks up on it and works on it as if it's his own project. You could say our brains are in contact somehow, that we instinctively know what the other is thinking. We realized this very early on. Arne was originally planning to start a company on his own. I was giving him advice and suggestions, and suddenly we were doing it together. It just happened.

IN WHAT WAYS ARE YOU ALIKE?
Carlos: We often like the same things. We are also both rather stubborn and will not hesitate to say what we think. This leads to lots of discussions, of course, but it is good if you can air your ideas.

IN WHAT WAYS ARE YOU DIFFERENT?
Carlos: Arne is very detail oriented, and I tend to look at the big picture more. Arne thinks of lots and lots of things and then I put his ideas in a context. When we are working on a book, Arne usually does the research and thinks of the items. Then we work together on the creative part and the design. After that, I structure everything and get the manuscript ready for the publisher. It is the ideal working method for us.

between them as well as harmony. "Sometimes, the relationships that most sustain us are also the relationships that most vex us," says Shenk. "I see that more clearly now. If you have an encounter and you walk away thinking, *That person makes me angry*, and it's agitating to you, don't discount that person. That's a primary mistake people make. Those people who are agitating to you, or who kind of get your blood up—that's a common quality of a great partner."

They must have time for the intensity of their creative process together, but then they also need to have time alone to

> ## The key element is to find a workable balance between connection and autonomy.

recharge, to explore their own individual part of the work. They also have to be willing to engage with one another, through both the harmonious and the very difficult moments—particularly through the difficult moments. If you're on the lookout for someone to collaborate with, Shenk says it's important to remember that emotions are a part of the equation.

FINDING "THE ONE." Shenk found that the key element to this kind of high-intensity collaboration is a workable balance between connection and autonomy.

He also cautions that creative partnerships sometimes only begin when both parties recognize the magic. "There's certainly that moment of fireworks, but not necessarily at the moment they meet," he says. But we can't wait for collaboration to create; we must create and find a collaborator who understands what we are doing. "All we can do is do our best to try to connect and find the work we want to do. If the moment arises for a primary partnership that challenges our ego and creates the condition for better work, then seize it."

THE IMAGE OF COLLABORATION.
When working on a project alone, it's easy to get so caught up in the process of creating that we forget to take a step back and explore all the facets of the project. Having a creative partner means having another set of eyes—and another perspective. A creative partner can also provide a sounding board for ideas: The simple act of verbalizing an idea to an objective person can allow you to clarify your own thoughts.

Then, by listening to his or her reactions, you not only gain a clearer image of the goal, but you also gain insight into what kind of impression or influence your work could have on others. Lastly, a creative collaborator offers accountability. Just like how it's easier to actually go to the gym if you know a friend is waiting there for you, having a creative partner provides motivation to keep working. Having that person who's invested in what you're doing will push you to stay on track.

"Coming together
is a beginning,
keeping together is progress,
working together is success."

—Henry Ford

ASTRID & IRENE: "OUR MINDS WORK IN SIMILAR WAYS."

The authors of this book, Astrid van der Hulst and Irene Smit, were coworkers at a different magazine when they dreamed up *Flow* magazine together. Now, they work closely together every day.

HOW DOES THE MAGIC BETWEEN YOU TWO WORK?

Astrid: The very first time we talked about what we would like to do with our careers, it turned out we had the same thoughts about magazines, paper, and all kinds of themes that were missing in the magazines that existed at the time. We also quickly found out that we are good at thinking up new concepts together. Irene says something, I finish her sentence, and then we quickly have a fully formed concept. I've never experienced that with anyone else.

IN WHAT WAYS ARE YOU ALIKE?

Astrid: We are flexible, and neither of us really has a nine-to-five mentality.

Irene: We both sense things, we're intuitive, and we're feelings people.

IN WHAT WAYS ARE YOU DIFFERENT?

Astrid: Irene is better at logistics, at practicalities, and in finding solutions. She also has more of a bionic editor's eye. I think I may be the more artistic of us two. I like commissioning illustrations and thinking of paper extras.

Irene: Astrid is more patient than I am. She can take the time to think through every detail of a foldable box diorama, for example, and work on it with an illustrator until it is really beautiful down to the last detail. I think I am better at stepping back for the broader overview of our company. In the end, the combination of the two of us working together is best.

AND NOW YOU

Make a list of collaborative projects you were part of in the past.
Who did you do these projects with? How did you work as a team?
What did you learn?

PROJECT 1:

PROJECT 2:

PROJECT 3:

_____

_____

_____

_____

_____

_____

PROJECT 4:

_____

_____

_____

_____

_____

PROJECT 5:

PROJECT 6:

ACKNOWLEDGMENTS

An enormous thank you to all the freelance journalists and artists whose contributions to our magazine form the foundation for this book.

ALL ART BY KATE PUGSLEY EXCEPT:
Pages 11, 25, 43, 55, 67, 83, 101, 117, 131, 147, 161, 175, 195: Shutterstock
Page 85: This circle is based on the book *How to Stay Sane* by Philippa Perry, published by The School of Life.
Pages 85, 87: Deborah van der Schaaf
Pages 112, 113: Amy Blackwell
Pages 176-183: Anisa Makhoul
Postcards: Danielle Kroll, Jennifer Orkin Lewis, Hanna Melin,
Sanny van Loon, Dick Vincent, Karen Weening
Posters: Getty Images

TEXT CREDITS:
Contributing writers: Fleur Baxmeier, Alice Binnendijk,
Caroline Buijs, Jocelyn de Kwant, Jeannette Jonker,
Francisca Kramer, Irene Ras, Nina Siegal, Sjoukje van de Kolk,
Otje van der Lelij, Renate van der Zee

ABOUT THE AUTHORS

Irene Smit and Astrid van der Hulst are the creative directors of *Flow* magazine, a popular international publication packed with paper goodies and beautiful illustrations celebrating creativity, imperfection, and life's little pleasures. Astrid and Irene began their magazine careers as editors at *Cosmopolitan* and *Marie Claire*. In 2008, inspired by their passion for paper and quest for mindfulness, Irene and Astrid dreamed up the idea for their own magazine in a small attic and haven't looked back since. They are also the authors of the bestselling *A Book That Takes Its Time*, *The Tiny Book of Tiny Pleasures*, *Everything Grows with Love*, and *50 Ways to Draw Your Beautiful, Ordinary Life*. They each live with their family in Haarlem, Netherlands.